TECHNOLOGY in WORLD HISTORY

2

EARLY EMPIRES

W. BERNARD CARLSON

Editor

OXFORD
UNIVERSITY PRESS

Contributing Editor:
Michael N. Geselowitz
Director, IEEE History Center, Rutgers University

Published in the United States of America by
Oxford University Press, Inc.
198 Madison Avenue
New York, NY 10016
www.oup.com

Oxford is a registered trademark of Oxford
University Press

Oxford University Press, Inc., publishes works
that further Oxford University's objective of
excellence in research, scholarship, and
education.

Oxford   New York
Auckland   Cape Town   Dar es Salaam
Hong Kong   Karachi   Kuala Lumpur
Madrid   Melbourne   Mexico City   Nairobi
New Delhi   Shanghai   Taipei   Toronto

With offices in
Argentina   Austria   Brazil   Chile   Czech
Republic   France   Greece   Guatemala
Hungary   Italy   Japan   Poland   Portugal
Singapore   South Korea   Switzerland
Thailand   Turkey   Ukraine   Vietnam

Project Directors *Susan Kennedy, Shaun Barrington*
Project Manager and Design *Steve McCurdy*
Editors *John Mapps, Andrew Solway, Angela
        Davies, Virginia Carter, Penny Isaac*
Cartographers *Richard Watts, Tim Williams*
Picture Manager *Claire Turner*
Picture Researcher *David Pratt*
Illustrations *Kevin Maddison*
Glossary *John O. E. Clark, W. Bernard Carlson,
        Paola Sanmiguel*
Production *Clive Sparling*

Volume ISBN-13: 978-0-19-521822-0
Volume ISBN-10: 0-19-521822-1

Printed in China

Library of Congress Cataloging-in-Publication data

Technology in world history / W. Bernard Carlson, editor.
    p. cm.
Includes bibliographical references and index.
    ISBN-13: 978-0-19-521820-6 (set: alk. paper)
    ISBN-10: 0-19-521820-5 (set: alk. paper)
    1. Technology and civilization. [1. Technology
and civilization.] I. Carlson, W. Bernard. II. Title.
    CB478.T3848 2003
    909--dc21
                        2003055300

CONTENTS

FOREWORD TO THIS SET

Thomas P. Hughes

MELLON PROFESSOR OF THE HISTORY AND SOCIOLOGY OF SCIENCE, EMERITUS, UNIVERSITY OF PENNSYLVANIA,
VISITING PROFESSOR, MASSACHUSETTS INSTITUTE OF TECHNOLOGY

An industrial scene depicted by the Flemish painter Joachim Patinier (c. 1475–1524). Ironworkers load iron ore into baskets and pour it into the top of the furnace.

People living in the modern, developed world tend to make a number of easy assumptions about the nature of technology and its role in history. They consider the complex and powerful technological systems that they use today to be superior to the machines and tools of their ancestors. People equate technology with progress, assuming that, as technology produces more goods, services, and information, human society will automatically improve. They expect greater material abundance to eradicate disease, hunger, and ignorance as well as promote greater human happiness and freedom. At the start of the 21st century, we would like to think that technology is the answer to most human needs and wants. Some historians have also held this view, and it has affected their analysis of world history.

But the role of technology in human history cannot be reduced solely to its ability to provide more easily the necessities of life—food, shelter and clean water—as well as consumer goods. Modern technology is not even necessarily superior to ancient technology. Using modern machinery, engineers today would find it difficult to build the pyramids as quickly and as precisely as the ancient Egyptians did 5,000 years ago. Likewise, centuries ago Pacific Islanders studied the form of sharks and other fish in order to design streamlined, fast-moving boats with complex hull shapes.

Technology does not always ensure human progress. Emperors in both Rome and China relied on engineers to build extensive road systems and equip their armies with sophisticated weapons, but such prowess did not prevent their societies from suffering invasion, epidemics, or famine. Nineteenth-century industrial cities in Europe and North America enjoyed greater wealth after the introduction of coal-fired steam engines but at the cost of air pollution and the suffering of factory workers who lived and labored in terrible conditions.

Most important, people do not develop technology simply in response to economic and material needs but also to realize social and spiritual aspirations. For instance, throughout the world today people are acquiring cellular telephones not just because they want to participate in the global economy, not just because giant corporations are selling this technology aggressively, but because they want to talk and socialize with friends and family. People use cell phones to sustain a sense of community. Medieval Europeans used their most advanced technology to construct magnificent cathedrals, as expressions of their religious faith. Similarly, the commercial and financial towers of Manhattan express their own set of modern values. Those buildings are not merely functional; they represent the beliefs of those who financed them, built them, and work in them about the primacy of the capitalist system.

Technology in World History seeks to explore how people have used technology to shape societies. By looking at cultures from around the world and across time, this set reveals not only the many different tools, machines, and systems that people have invented but also the remarkable array of uses to which they have applied technology. Again and again, readers will discover that people have created technology not only to satisfy material needs but also in response to political ideas and spiritual beliefs. In fact, although all human cultures have some form of technology, every culture uses its technology in different ways. By looking at technologies past and present, East and West, these volumes should help the reader to appreciate the many ways humans have used technology and understand the implications of our present attitudes toward technological development.

USING THIS SET

Technology describes the knowledge and range of skills that humans employ to make the things they use. All human societies use technology to provide themselves with food, clothing, and shelter. They make tools and produce useful or decorative objects. But every society uses technology in different ways to express cultural ideas about how that society is organized and what gives life spiritual or religious meaning. For example, some cultures employ technology to concentrate wealth in the hands of a ruling class, whereas others choose to distribute wealth and power more equally among all members of society. People construct great monuments such as temples, cathedrals, and skyscrapers as expressions of their ideas about sacred, political, or economic power. They develop different ways of communicating ideas, of spreading information, and of organizing knowledge.

The intention of this set is not to suggest that some technologies—or some societies—are better than others. Rather, it sets out to reveal something of the amazing array of tools,

machines, systems, and practices that people have created in order to survive and thrive on Earth and to explore the various ways in which people have used technology to establish and maintain societies over the centuries. To do this, each of the six main volumes looks at three distinct cultures. The eighteen featured technologies extend in time from the Stone Age to the present day and stretch around the globe. The chapters do not attempt to provide a comprehensive history of civilization from the earliest times to the present. Instead, they concentrate on a number of societies in which people have utilized technology in powerful and unusual ways to shape their culture.

First and foremost, humans have relied on technology to produce food and wealth—the material abundance necessary to sustain the population. Experts think of this as the economic function of technology. In each chapter you will find information about how different societies provided food for themselves and about the materials—stone, wood, mud, and clay, metals such as copper, bronze, and iron, and fibers and textiles—they used to fashion clothing, shelter, and objects for daily use. The chapters

Summary of main points provided at the beginning of each chapter

Some illustrations show how people represented their own technologies in art

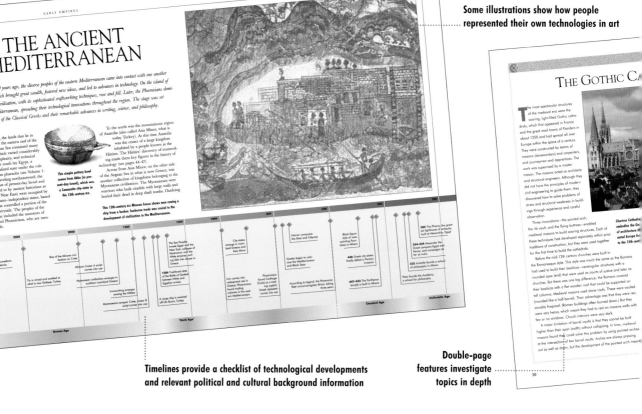

Timelines provide a checklist of technological developments and relevant political and cultural background information

Double-page features investigate topics in depth

examine the means—the tools, machinery, sources of power and forms of transportation—used to manufacture and distribute goods and to create wealth.

Although food, shelter, and clothing are necessary for human existence, they do not guarantee that people will be happy or safe. This set also considers how people rely on technology to achieve noneconomic goals—to organize society, confer social status, provide pleasure, and deploy political power. We are all aware that people like to have technological gadgets and the latest models not just because these items are practical but because they convey messages about the person who uses them.

As with individuals, so it is with societies. Whether building the Egyptian pyramids or developing the American space program, societies clearly use technology for a variety of noneconomic reasons to express complex ideas about themselves and their beliefs. The pyramids are both an expression of religious beliefs and of the power of the ruling pharaohs. The space program is a symbol of the human pioneering spirit and was also—particularly during the Cold War era when the Soviet Union and the United States were in perpetual readiness for war with each other—an indicator of technological supremacy. Technology interacts with the myths, religion, art, and philosophy of a culture.

It is always tempting to ask "What if?" in the history of technology. What if the 17th-century mathematical genius Sir Isaac Newton had owned a personal computer? Might his investigations have led him to discover nuclear physics and invent the atomic bomb? What if the Maya had possessed rockets? Would their advanced astronomy have let them travel into space centuries ago? The truth is that, even if it were possible for specific technological devices to travel back through time in some mysterious way, they are unlikely to have changed the course of history. This is because the individuals living in past societies would have found that modern machines had no connection to the ideas, values, or beliefs of their own culture. Major inventions such as the steam engine or the computer chip did not make history; instead, people used and shaped these technologies in pursuit of their society's beliefs and goals.

The volumes in this series are arranged chronologically, though any of the three chapters in each volume can be read alone, without reference to the other chapters. **Timelines** help set technological innovations in historical context. **Maps** provide a concise record of the geographical spread of new technologies. **Feature boxes** look in depth at specific topics, from the development of the alphabet to marine archaeology. Each volume has its own **index**, and the reference volume provides a complete **set index**, together with an extensive **glossary**. If any technical terms in the text are unfamiliar, the glossary will help explain them.

Diagrams explain the technological principles at work

Maps show the spread of technology

Photographs of historical artifacts pinpoint key breakthroughs

INTRODUCTION
EARLY EMPIRES

In 221 BCE a leader named Shihuangdi (259–210 BCE), from the western Chinese state of Qin, created a unified China by conquering all of the rival warring states. Bringing to an end nearly four centuries of constant warfare, Shihuangdi declared himself emperor and boldly predicted that his successors would rule China for 10,000 generations.

But how should Shihuangdi consolidate his power and create a unified Chinese culture? Having achieved victory on the battlefield by using mass-produced crossbows and new cavalry tactics, it is perhaps not surprising that Shihuangdi turned to technology. First, to protect the empire's western border, Shihuangdi dispatched 300,000 workers to build the Great Wall. Next, to eliminate any future rivals from gaining too much power inside China, he abolished the old system of aristocratic fiefdoms and instead divided his empire into 36 districts, each headed by a civil governor, a military commander, and an imperial inspector.

To permit his officials and troops to travel to the far-flung districts and enforce his rule, Shihuangdi built a network of roads radiating from his capital at Xianyang. To ensure that imperial pronouncements would be obeyed, Shihuangdi ordered that everything be standardized, including the law, language, taxes, weights, and measures. Shihuangdi issued standard copper coins with a square hole in the center, and he insisted that the axle width of all carts be the same. Shihuangdi's engineers accomplished this by cutting ruts at the official width in the roads for the wheels of the carts. Shihuangdi understood well that technology could be used to demonstrate political power, and upon his death he was buried in an elaborate tomb guarded by 7,000 life-size terra-cotta soldiers.

This volume explores how different groups followed Shihuangdi's example and used technology to create empires between 2000 BCE and 500 CE. The story begins with ancient China, where civilization grew up in the fertile valleys of the Yellow and Yangtze Rivers. Early on, the Chinese demonstrated great technical ingenuity by casting bronze bells and ceremonial vessels and by manufacturing crossbows with interchangeable trigger mechanisms.

The volume's middle chapter surveys several empires that rose and fell around the Mediterranean Sea: the Minoans, Hittites, Phoenicians, and classical Greeks. These cultures thrived as a result of developing better ships, iron tools and weapons, and new goods such as olive oil, wine, and dyes for trade. Drawing on their economic success as farmers and traders, the Greeks could devote their energy to the development of political theory and scientific thought. Following the conquests of Alexander the Great (356–323 BCE), Greek ideas spread throughout the Mediterranean world and eventually came to influence an up-and-coming city-state called Rome.

The last chapter shows how the Romans used technology to sustain their empire and society. Believing that their strength came from being a nation of farmers and soldiers, the Romans chose to concentrate much of their technological effort on improving agriculture and weapons. Like the Chinese, the Romans standardized their laws and language and built a network of roads that permitted troops to move quickly between the capital and the provinces. Because Romans also saw the state as a commonwealth—responsible for providing for the common good—both the emperor and leading citizens served as patrons for major engineering projects such as aqueducts, temples, public baths, and sports arenas. This was not just generosity or public spiritedness: being able to pay for massive public buildings was an outward show of political power and wealth.

Enjoying political stability for several centuries, the Romans generated a number of devices still used today. Collectively, then, this volume reveals the many ways in which people (such as the Romans) and rulers (such as Shihuangdi) have employed technology to exercise political power and create strong, enduring states.

The Altar of Augustan Peace, commissioned by the emperor Augustus in 13 BCE.
(See page 70)

EARLY CHINA

A distinctive Chinese civilization grew from a nucleus of ancient farming cultures settled around the Yellow and Yangtze Rivers. Between 4,000 and 3,000 years ago, the people of this region began to live in towns and to produce bronze vessels. Technologies became ever more sophisticated, setting the stage for the extraordinary achievements of the first Chinese empires, the Qin and Han, a little more than 2,000 years ago.

The fertile northern plains along the Yellow River were the heartland of the cultural and political tradition that eventually came to be known as Chinese. This region is where the early ruling dynasties of China had their capital cities. There, too, the Chinese script first developed in the 2nd millennium BCE. Chinese historical texts traditionally speak of three ancient dynasties as having ruled in the northern plains of China—the Xia, the Shang, and the Zhou. According to the old chronologies, the Xia dynasty ruled from about 2000 to 1650 BCE, the Shang from about 1650 to 1050 BCE, and the Zhou from about 1050 to 221 BCE.

Until 1928, the Zhou dynasty was the first for which there was documentary evidence. Later generations looked back on the Zhou as a golden age. Around 770 BCE Zhou authority weakened, leading to a period of disorder known as the

Bronze objects, such as this Sanxingdui face mask, are evidence that complex civilizations using sophisticated technology had taken shape in China by at least 1500 BCE.

Spring and Autumn period (770–481 BCE). When the authority of the Zhou kings finally crumbled, former vassal states of the Zhou began attacking each other and neighboring states during a time of almost constant warfare called the Warring States period (480–221 BCE). It ended when Shihuangdi (Chinese for the First Emperor) unified the whole of China and founded the short-lived Qin dynasty (221–206 BCE).

After a brief civil war, the Han dynasty (206 BCE–220 CE) took power, marking the true beginnings of imperial rule. It was during this period that the northern heartland on the Yellow River came to be identified as *Zhongguo* (meaning "the Central States"), rendered as *China* in English. The people of this heartland were part of a mosaic of races and language groups who had inhabited the region of east Asia for a considerable time.

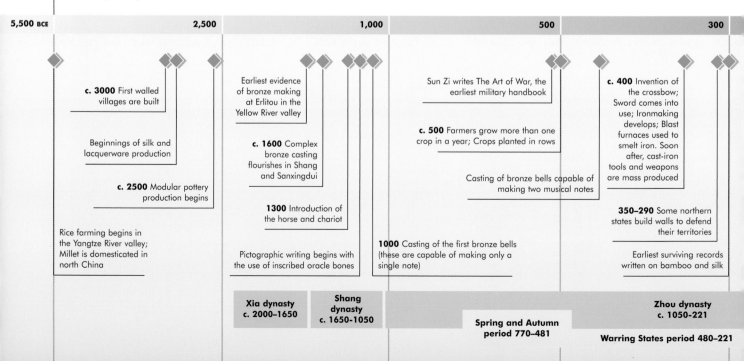

5,500 BCE	2,500	1,000	500	300

c. 3000 First walled villages are built

Beginnings of silk and lacquerware production

c. 2500 Modular pottery production begins

Rice farming begins in the Yangtze River valley; Millet is domesticated in north China

Earliest evidence of bronze making at Erlitou in the Yellow River valley

c. 1600 Complex bronze casting flourishes in Shang and Sanxingdui

1300 Introduction of the horse and chariot

Pictographic writing begins with the use of inscribed oracle bones

Sun Zi writes The Art of War, the earliest military handbook

c. 500 Farmers grow more than one crop in a year; Crops planted in rows

Casting of bronze bells capable of making two musical notes

1000 Casting of the first bronze bells (these are capable of making only a single note)

c. 400 Invention of the crossbow; Sword comes into use; Ironmaking develops; Blast furnaces used to smelt iron. Soon after, cast-iron tools and weapons are mass produced

350–290 Some northern states build walls to defend their territories

Earliest surviving records written on bamboo and silk

Xia dynasty c. 2000–1650

Shang dynasty c. 1650-1050

Spring and Autumn period 770–481

Zhou dynasty c. 1050-221

Warring States period 480–221

EARLY TECHNOLOGY

The transition from hunting–gathering to settled farming took place much later in east Asia than in the Near East and Egypt. The earliest cultures of the Neolithic period (New Stone Age) in China date back not much further than 5000 or 6000 BCE, some 3,000 years later than in the Near East, while the earliest Bronze Age urban centers appeared in the early 2nd millennium BCE, 2,000 years after the Mesopotamians began making bronze. The Chinese began using iron in the 5th century BCE, about 500 years later than in the West (see Volume 2, pages 48–49).

Because so many technical innovations appeared later in China than in the Near East,

Cultivated fields on the banks of the Yellow River form a checkerboard pattern. This fertile region formed the heartland of the early Chinese state.

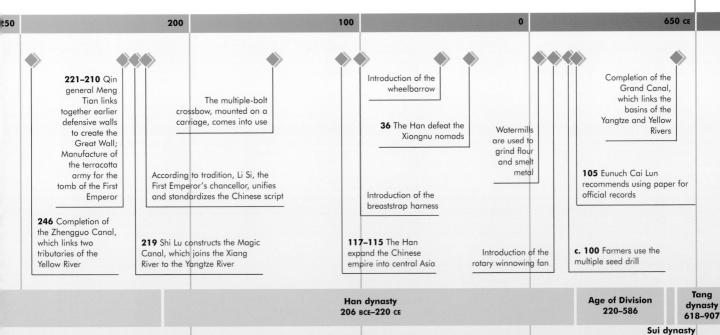

250	200	100	0	650 CE

221–210 Qin general Meng Tian links together earlier defensive walls to create the Great Wall; Manufacture of the terracotta army for the tomb of the First Emperor

The multiple-bolt crossbow, mounted on a carriage, comes into use

Introduction of the wheelbarrow

36 The Han defeat the Xiongnu nomads

Watermills are used to grind flour and smelt metal

Completion of the Grand Canal, which links the basins of the Yangtze and Yellow Rivers

According to tradition, Li Si, the First Emperor's chancellor, unifies and standardizes the Chinese script

Introduction of the breaststrap harness

105 Eunuch Cai Lun recommends using paper for official records

246 Completion of the Zhengguo Canal, which links two tributaries of the Yellow River

219 Shi Lu constructs the Magic Canal, which joins the Xiang River to the Yangtze River

117–115 The Han expand the Chinese empire into central Asia

Introduction of the rotary winnowing fan

c. 100 Farmers use the multiple seed drill

Han dynasty 206 BCE–220 CE

Age of Division 220–586

Tang dynasty 618–907

Sui dynasty 581–618

⊗ WRITING

The oldest true written Chinese texts are found on oracle bones of the Shang dynasty. The early Shang kings used the bony under-shells of turtles or the shoulder blades of cattle or sheep to communicate with their ancestors. Royal diviners struck these oracle bones with a hot metal rod and interpreted the resulting pattern of cracks to give the ancestors' answers to questions posed by the living regarding future events. By about 1350 BCE, oracle bones were engraved with texts recording both the questions and the answers.

The writing on Shang period oracle bones already used the full-fledged Chinese script system. This employs true pictographs (for example, simplified depictions of a tree or a mountain) and ideographs—symbols such as a man with his arms outstretched to represent "large," or a roof over a pig to signify "house." However, most Chinese characters are compounds of phonetic (sounded) and semantic (signifying) elements. For example, the character for "pear," a word that is pronounced *li*, combines the element signifying wood or tree with the character meaning "benefit," also pronounced *li*. These phonetic-

Modern Chinese script evolved from symbols carved on Shang oracle bones. These characters both mean "tree." The upper one is Shang, the lower one, modern. Modern Chinese has about 40,000 characters, of which 10,000 are in common use.

semantic compounds were already used in writing the oracle bone texts. The Shang and Zhou also wrote inscriptions on ritual bronzes, which have survived in great numbers. Apart from ritual purposes, writing—in tandem with methods of record-keeping and accounting—was also a key technique for mobilizing the vast numbers of laborers who constructed fortifications and palaces, tilled the royal farmlands, and made the prestige and everyday goods required by the ruling class and their servants.

Some early texts were written in a different script and possibly a different language from Chinese. According to tradition, Li Si, the First Emperor's chancellor, unified and standardized the Chinese script soon after the unification of the empire in 221 BCE. Imperial officials were expected to have a good education and have access to plenty of books. This was particularly important for any technical enterprise, such as running the imperial factories, improving local agriculture, or conducting military campaigns.

At first, the Chinese wrote on silk textiles and wooden or bamboo slips. Although paper was made in China from at least the 2nd century BCE, the Chinese appear at first to have used it for wrapping items rather than for writing. Cai Lun, a court official, is credited with inventing paper in 105 CE, but in fact he recommended that paper be used for imperial record-keeping because it was cheaper than silk and lighter than bamboo. The Han Chinese made paper from silk rags, pulped in water, and then formed into thin sheets. (See Volume 3: Late Imperial China, page 67, for more on Chinese paper.)

This oracle bone dates from the 14th or 13th century BCE. Rulers used oracle bones to ask their ancestors questions about the outcome of an illness, the timing of a military campaign, the success of a harvest, and so on. Writing developed to record what the ancestors foretold.

Western scholars in the late 19th and early 20th centuries argued that advancements, ranging from knowledge of farming and pottery to metalworking, must have been introduced to China from the West. Recent archaeological discoveries suggest otherwise.

Until about 50 years ago, Chinese texts, written many hundreds of years ago and transmitted with varying degrees of accuracy down the centuries, were the main source of

information for the early history of China. These ancient texts dealt only very lightly with the material conditions of life and provided scanty evidence about technical developments.

Scholars believed that the first two of the three Chinese dynasties mentioned in the histories, the Xia and Shang dynasties, were legends because there was no material evidence to show that they had ever existed. But a stunning discovery made in 1928 changed this

Machanggou

Inner
Mongolian
Plateau

Luan

QIAN MTS

Lijiacun
Xiadu

Liyu

Korea
Bay

Sanggan

Liaodong
Peninsula

Baode

Ordos
Desert

HELAN MTS

Pingshan

Taixicun

Bo Hai

Shandong
Peninsula

Tengger
Desert

BAIYU MTS

Suide

Fen

Shilou

Sufutun

LULIANG MTS

Xingtai

Ji'nan

Linzi

LIUPAN MTS

Houma

Handan

Lingshanwei

Dongxiang

Xiang

Anyang

Zhang

Yellow

Qufu

Yellow
Sea

Jing

Jiang

Huixian

Chaoge

Cao

TAIHANG MTS

Shan

Fei Huang

Shan

Zhengzhou

Fengxiang
Qishan

Yellow

Xinzheng

Shangqiu

Qin

Wei

Baoji

Fufeng

Hao

Luoyang
Erlitou
(Zhenling)

Chen

L. Hongze

L. Gaoyou

QIN MTS

Ying

Huai

L. Chao

L. Tai

MIN MTS

Han

Xincai

Yangtze

Gusu

MICANG
MTS

DABA MTS

Leigudun

DABIE MTS

Yangtze

QIONGLAI MTS

Jialing

Jingshan

Panlongcheng

Han

Zhuji

Pengxian

Sanxingdui
Juliandun

Ying

Fuchun

Qu

Fu

Sichuan Basin

Yangtze

Wu

Min

Tao

Yangtze

DALOU MTS

Zi

WULING
MTS

Yuan

Ningxiang

MUFU MTS

L. Dongting

L. Poyang

Wucheng
Xinjian

East
China
Sea

Xiang

Gan

Xingan

WUYI MTS

Da

(see pages 16–20)

point of view. Archaeologists digging at Anyang in modern-day Henan province uncovered the site of a huge city, including the remains of palaces, temples, and altars. They unearthed numerous inscribed bronze artifacts. These made it clear that Anyang was the capital city of the Shang dynasty, so providing documentary proof that the Shang emperors had indeed existed. The traditional histories relate that the Shang rulers moved to their capital city in about 1400 BCE; the latest archaeological evidence suggests that Anyang was founded about 1350 BCE.

Archaeologists have since excavated urban centers in other parts of northern China where bronze vessels were being produced on a large scale for use in rituals (see pages 16–20) at an earlier date than in Anyang. Archaeologists now date the Shang period to between about 1650 and 1050 BCE. Some urban sites excavated in China were occupied before 1650 BCE. Scholars

think they may belong to the Xia civilization but there is no conclusive proof of this dynasty's existence. However, it is now generally agreed that the three ancient dynasties did not follow one after the other, but overlapped in time, and held sway in different regions of north China.

Archaeologists today have a much clearer image of the late prehistory and early history of the region that is now called China than earlier scholars did. They have also learned about China's relations with neighboring regions in east Asia (such as Vietnam and Korea), and with the wider world. It seems clear that some important technologies, such as the horse-drawn chariot and the cultivation of wheat, did indeed reach China from the West. However, many key technologies, such as the domestication of millet and rice and the development of pottery, as well as local traditions of bronze and iron technology, emerged independently in east Asia.

The heartland of Chinese civilization

- ▫ Shang site
- ▫ Zhou site
- —— area of Shang bronze-working
- ■ Zhou heartland (Zhouyuan)
- ■ maximum extent of Zhou dynasty
- ■ extent of Chinese cultural influence, 5th century BCE

0   300 km
0   200 mi

This map shows the known extent of Chinese influence during the Shang and Zhou dynasties. It is based on archaeologists' studies of bronze inscriptions found in numerous sites in the Yellow River region of northern China, as well as later histories.

⊗ ARCHAEOLOGY IN CHINA

Over the last 30 years, a number of archaeological discoveries in China have transformed our understanding of early Chinese technology and society. The Chinese government encourages archaeology and has a national network of archaeological bureaus. The state has also initiated numerous large construction projects, which have led to many archaeological discoveries as workers digging foundations come across ancient remains. Such projects have recently multiplied, creating a stream of new discoveries.

Most excavations are comparatively modest, but some are truly spectacular. For example, in 1989 archaeologists discovered a walled city at Sanxingdui in Sichuan province, which contained rich and exotic bronzes, many of a type never seen before (see page 8), as well as Shang-type artifacts. Most dramatic of all was the discovery, in 1974, of an army of thousands of life-size terracotta warriors near the burial mound of Shihuangdi, the First Emperor, who died in 210 BCE (see pages 27–28). Much work remains to be done at this site—an estimated 5,000 warriors are yet to be excavated—and Shihuangdi's burial mound is untouched.

The volume of evidence now available has given archaeologists a far richer understanding of early Chinese technology, including a few surprising challenges to conventional views of technical development. For instance, experts now argue that the development of iron production in China followed a technical path quite different from that typical of early western Asia, Europe, or Africa, starting not with village forges but with mass production organized by the state (see page 19). Tombs from the centuries just before and after the establishment of the Qin empire (3rd century BCE) have yielded an abundance of documents written on sheets of silk or bamboo slips. These documents include early versions of works of philosophy, cosmology, medicine, astronomy, and divination, together with legal codes, accounts, and manufacturing records. Weapons, textiles, and other artifacts inscribed with serial numbers have also been found. All these items have much to tell us about how goods were manufactured, controlled, and circulated in the early Chinese empire.

Excavation of a Zhou dynasty burial pit at Liulige in Hebei province revealed the remains of chariots and horses. Such discoveries provide archaeologists with vital information about technology and society in early China.

FARMING AND FOOD

In the 6th millennium BCE, Neolithic farmers in the northern plateaus and plains surrounding the Yellow River domesticated two kinds of millet (foxtail and broomcorn), while people living along the many rivers of the Yangtze Basin in the semitropical south domesticated rice. These separate events established two distinct farming traditions in China: in the south, irrigated rice-growing, and in the north, dry-field farming of millet, wheat, and barley.

Farmers in both regions domesticated chickens, pigs, and dogs at about the same time. By approximately 3000 BCE, sheep and cattle were common in the north, and cattle and water buffalo common in the south. The domesticated horse seems to have reached China from western Asia, along with the chariot, in about 1200 BCE. The Xiongnu nomads (known in the West as the Huns), who skirmished along China's northwestern border during the Han dynasty, introduced the donkey to China.

Rice is the domesticated form of the grass *Oryza sativa*, which grows naturally in swampland, and it therefore needs warm, moist conditions in which to grow. The earliest rice farmers planted this crop in low-lying marshes near rivers. Soon, however, rice farming expanded beyond the limited area of natural swamps. Rice farmers began to construct bunds (low dikes) around their fields to keep in rainwater during the growing season. Flooded fields used to grow rice are called paddies.

Rice was the primary source of wealth for the powerful states (Chu, Wu, Yue, Ba, and Shu) that arose during the 1st millennium BCE in the southern provinces. As early as the Warring States period, farmers in the kingdoms of Wu and Yue reclaimed large tracts of floodlands in river deltas for rice cultivation. First, a polder (high dike) was built encircling the land, then bunds were used to subdivide the land inside into small fields. Little canals ran between the fields, linked to the river by sluices (gates) in the dike. Farmers used the canals to flood the paddies when the young rice plants were grow-ing and to drain off water from the paddies shortly before harvesting.

Rice farmers also built holding tanks or reservoirs for storing water to irrigate their paddies. Pottery models of tanks found in Han dynasty graves indicate that tank irrigation was by then routine in the southern coastal provinces, around what is now Guangdong province and northern Vietnam. The labor-saving shaduf, a counterbalanced pole used for raising buckets of water from a well or a stream (see Volume 1: Ancient Egypt, page 54), appears to have reached China from western Asia by the 5th century BCE.

Rice remains the staple crop of southern China today. Some experts believe that the climate of the northern plains was warmer and more humid during the Shang dynasty than it is today so that, at that time, rice was a common crop there, too. However, northern farmers had certainly ceased growing it by the imperial period, and later official attempts to introduce rice cultivation in the northern provinces failed.

From earliest times Chinese farmers used their fields almost exclusively to grow grain, which they supplemented with vegetables grown in garden plots. They kept pigs and chickens in the yard, and raised fish and ducks in paddy fields or ponds. Children cut fodder (grass and weeds) from dikes and ditches to feed the oxen or buffalo used as draft animals, or led the animals to mountain pastures to graze. Every farmer devoted some land to either hemp or ramie, fiber crops that provided clothing for ordinary people. In some regions mulberry trees were grown to feed silkworms, the larvae of the silkworm moth. The silkworm makes a cocoon of silk (see page 25).

Land ownership

We do not know a great deal about the organi-zation of farming in China's very early states. Under the Zhou dynasty (c. 1050–221 BCE) the land was divided into estates owned by aristocrats and worked by peasant farmers. The nobles held their land as fiefs (gifts) from the king, and in exchange provided him with local products yearly, as well as an agreed number of peasant soldiers when he needed a fighting force. Warfare was almost constant between rival states during the Warring States period at the end of the Zhou. To survive, a state needed strong peasants to provide the ruler with an army, and full granaries to feed them. Political treatises written at this time give much thought to ways of improving farming.

Rice has been grown in southern China for about 7,000 years. It remains the staple crop today, cultivated in flooded paddy fields using centuries-old techniques.

The Qin state had risen to strength by abolishing aristocratic fiefs, introducing private ownership of land and direct official taxation of the peasants. When the Qin ruler united China in 221 BCE, he imposed this system throughout China. Peasant households paid taxes of one bushel of grain and one bolt of cloth yearly for each man and woman of working age in the family. Male peasants had to give regular periods of service to the state for building roads, canals, palaces, or defensive walls, and to fight in time of war. This system of ownership and taxation gave the emperor direct control of agricultural resources. Although feudal-type estates did emerge at times when central government was weak, strong emperors and ministers disbanded these landholdings, redistributed land in small parcels to peasants, and tried to control the growth of fiefs or landlord holdings.

Improvements in farming

The active interest taken by rulers and officials in promoting and improving agriculture led to many important technical advances. Most peasant farmers, on whom the imperial government depended for its tax base, lived in the northern provinces, where millet was the staple crop. The earliest written texts on farming methods deal with northern crop systems, and most government measures undertaken to improve agriculture targeted northern regions.

An anthology of ancient poems indicates that during the early Zhou dynasty fields in northern China were often cultivated in only one out of every two or three years, and left fallow (unplanted) in intervening years to recover their fertility. But by the Warring States period (480–221 BCE) it was common for farmers to cultivate fields continuously, sometimes growing three crops in two years by alternating winter- and spring-planted crops. Farmers planted millets in spring and harvested them in fall. By the Han period (206 BCE–220 CE) wheat and barley were popular winter-sown crops, harvested in late summer. Crop rotations often alternated nutrient-greedy crops such as cereals or oil-seeds with

This stone relief from a Han tomb shows two oxen drawing a plow. Ox-drawn metal plowshares (cutting blades) allowed farmers to plow more land and cut deeper furrows in heavier soils than ever before.

soil-enriching crops such as soybeans and other legumes (beans or peas).

Farmers fertilized their fields with compost made of animal manure supplemented with human excrement. Other methods of fertilization included plowing in weeds and stubble, and the use of green manure—planting a quick-growing, nitrogen-fixing crop such as beans or alfalfa and plowing it in before it ripened. All these techniques increased both the soil's fertility and its capacity to retain moisture, which was crucial in the low-rainfall regions of northern China.

Another important technique was row-cultivation. Farmers plowed their fields with alternating ridges and

A farmer operates a trip-hammer (a hammer mounted on the end of a wooden shaft) to pound grain in this ceramic model found in a tomb dating from the Han era. To the left of the farmer is a stone grain-mill.

furrows, and planted the seed at carefully spaced intervals along the ridges. At first they made the rows with hoes, the blades of which were made of bone or stone and attached to wooden handles. A form of ox-drawn plow probably came into use in parts of China in late Neolithic times. Iron plowshares (cutting blades) were in use by the Warring States period. By the 3rd century BCE, state factories were mass-producing various types of iron plow-shares for different soil types. The factories were also making mold-boards, curved plates of iron fitted over the blade so that it did not simply break the surface of the soil but turned it over as the plow moved forward. Farmers in Europe only began using this advanced form of plowing in medieval times (see Volume 3: Medieval Europe, page 11).

Han farmers used seed-drills to sow in straight lines. Seed-drills were first used in Mesopotamia and were probably introduced to China from western Asia through central Asia at the beginning of the imperial period (around 200 BCE). These devices, pulled by oxen, consisted of a box containing the seed, which fed into two, or sometimes three, tubes fitted with tiny iron blades. The blades cut straight, shallow trenches, and the farmer tilted the drill from one side to another as it moved forward, releasing the seed down each tube in turn. This produced regular, staggered rows of plants. As one Chinese writer in the 3rd century BCE put it: "If crops are grown in rows they will mature rapidly because they will not interfere with each other's growth. The horizontal rows must be well drawn, the vertical rows made with skill, for if the lines are straight the wind will pass gently through."

Imperial experts wrote texts encouraging the spread of intensive farming techniques. These methods could be put into practice only on large farms because they depended on farmers having oxen as draft animals and a wide range of equipment, such as rollers that compacted the soil to retain moisture from frost or snow. On small farms, peasants husked grain by pounding it in a mortar. On large farms, farmers used a device known as a trip hammer, consisting of a hammer set at one end of a long shaft. The operator pushed a foot treadle to depress the the other end of the shaft, so raising the hammer, and released it to let the hammer fall on the grain. Water-driven wheels powered sets of trip-hammers by the late Han period. As a water-wheel turned, it activated a lug or handle mounted on an axle, which automatically depressed the shafts of the trip-hammers.

Han farmers employed rotary winnowing fans to separate the light chaff (husks and pieces of stalk) from the heavier grain. These fans were among the earliest machinery to make use of a crank, a winding handle attached to an axle. The fan consisted of six or eight wooden vanes mounted on an axle, set at one end of a horizontal wooden shaft. The shaft was open at the other end. At the top of the shaft, between the fan and the open end, was a hopper or funnel into which one worker poured the threshed grain. Another worker turned the crank, creating a fierce draft of air that blew the chaff away out of the end of the shaft, while the grain, which was heavier than the chaff, fell down into an outlet directly below the hopper, and was collected in a basket.

Food preparation

Grains—rice, millet, wheat, barley—and vegetables made up most of the Chinese diet. Ordinary Chinese ate little meat, and no dairy products.

Rice and millet grains were husked and steamed whole. This practice seems to have begun very early. Archaeologists have found that many Neolithic Chinese cultures used a distinctive form of pottery grain-steamer with three legs. These tripods are also found in early dynastic sites, both in pottery form for everyday use, and in bronze for use by the wealthy in ancestral rituals.

The Chinese fermented certain types of millet and rice to make alcoholic beverages. These brews are usually referred to as wines, though in fact they are more like beers. Special beakers and goblets for pouring and drinking wine were also made in bronze for ritual use.

This Shang bronze vessel, known as a *jue*, held an alcoholic beverage made from fermented millet. The "wine" was drunk at feasts and offered to the ancestors.

The Chinese used handmills to grind wheat and barley into flour, which they made into bread or noodles. During the Han dynasty, the Chinese developed water-powered flour mills. Moving water turned a large wooden wheel, which rotated a shaft connected to a millstone. The turning millstone ground the grain to flour against a stationary stone. Watermills and handmills also ground soybeans to a pulp that was fermented to make sauces and pickles.

BRONZE: THE BADGE OF EARLY RULE

Bronze, an alloy (mixture) of copper and tin, began to be produced in China around 1700 BCE. At first, bronzeworkers made rather light and thin vessels, but by the late Shang dynasty, and through the Zhou dynasty, they were casting enormous objects. The largest known is a rectangular food cauldron from the Shang capital of Anyang. It is 52 inches (132 cm) high and just under 2,000 pounds (900 kg) in weight. Such vessels gave great status to their aristocratic owners; other classes were banned from possessing bronze and other luxury goods such as lacquerware (see page 25).

At the ritual feasts central to Shang court life, members of ruling families communed with the spirits of their ancestors—who they believed could directly influence their lives—or conducted politics with other nobles. Guests ate and drank from bronze rice-steamers, cauldrons, beakers, and goblets. Before the feast, musicians played solemn music on bronze bells and other instruments to summon the ancestral spirits to join the festivities.

Sometimes a noble would have a bronze vessel specially cast to celebrate an achievement that brought honor to the family line, such as a victory in battle or the bestowing of a higher rank by the king. An inscription on the vessel recorded the circumstances of its casting, together with wishes for the owner's long life and many descendants. Kings bestowed vessels on their nobles; lesser nobles gave vessels as tribute to

the more powerful; noble houses exchanged vessels as gifts to cement alliances.

Many bronze pieces were handed down from generation to generation, but it was also customary to bury bronzes with the dead. Graves often included as many as 200 bronze items. One tomb excavated at Anyang belonging to Lady Hao, the wife of King Wu Ding, who died around 1250 BCE, contained more than 400 bronze artifacts, which had a combined weight of more than a ton. Nearly half the vessels had a ritual purpose.

Bronze bells

In the late 1970s, archaeologists excavated the tomb of Marquis Yi—ruler of Zeng, a small state located in what is now Hubei province—who died in about 433 BCE. In the tomb's main chamber, representing the hall where the marquis would have performed his ritual duties as a ruler, the excavators found the remains of a complete ritual orchestra including a set of 65 bronze bells with gold-inlaid inscriptions.

Sets of bronze bells were part of royal orchestras as early as the Shang dynasty. During the early part of the Zhou dynasty, only the king was entitled to hang rows of these instruments on all four sides of the courtyard of his ancestral temple. Feudal lords were entitled to three rows, ministers to two rows on opposite sides of the courtyard, and ordinary noblemen to a single row. The early Chinese believed that music was not only the medium for communicating with ancestral spirits, but also a potent instrument of government by which the ruler mediated between human society and the cosmos. They believed that when music was played inside the palace, its vibrations spread social harmony throughout the realm.

The set of bells found in the tomb of Marquis Yi illustrates the sophistication of Zhou bronze-casting techniques. In cross section, each bell is elliptical, rather than circular, making it possible to obtain two musical notes depending on where the bell is struck. The knobs on the outside of the bells improved resonance. The figurine at right supports the lacquered wooden stand on which the bells hang.

⊗ BRONZEMAKING TECHNOLOGY

To make bronze, metalworkers first melt ores of copper and tin under intense heat to extract the metal content. They then mix the metals together in proportions of roughly two-thirds copper to one-third tin, rising in some cases to 90 percent copper and 10 percent tin (this process is known as smelting). Bronze resembles pure metals like gold, silver, or copper in many respects. Like them, it is shiny and colorful, and it can be formed into many shapes by being hammered, or by being melted and cast (poured) into molds. Bronze has an added quality: it is relatively hard and can be sharpened to an edge. Therefore, bronze was useful not just for making jewelry, vessels, armor, and display objects—early societies also used it to manufacture weapons.

Bronze was first made in the Near East around 3500 BCE, some 2,000 years before it was made in China. However, scholars today have no doubt that bronzemaking technology developed independently in early China and did not spread there from outside. Shang and Zhou bronzeworkers cast their bronzes in a very different way to those of other ancient civilizations. Metalworkers in western Asia and in neighboring parts of east Asia (present-day Vietnam and Cambodia) made bronze objects by hammering them into shape, or by the lost-wax process. This process involves making a wax model of the object to be cast, then coating the model with clay (see picture, below left). The bronzeworker placed the

clay model in an oven. The wax melted, flowing out through small drainpipes, leaving a cavity behind. The worker poured liquid bronze into the cavity. When the bronze hardened, he broke the clay mold to release the bronze object.

Shang and Zhou bronzeworkers, however, cast their bronzes using a much more elaborate method known as the piece-mold process, sometimes described as "casting bronze the complicated way." The casting methods involved not one, but several workers. One worker made a clay model of the object to be cast and fired it in a kiln. Others applied a layer of wet clay to the outer surface of the finished model, and removed it in several sections. They fired these sections in the kiln to form the outer mold. Then they clamped the pieces of the outer mold together around a clay core in the shape of the final object, poured molten bronze into the space between the mold and the core, and left it to harden (see picture, below right).

The lost-wax method was introduced to China during the late Zhou period. It allowed craftsmen to produce pierced or open filigree designs. Sometimes they used both the lost-wax and piece-mold methods in combination to make a single object.

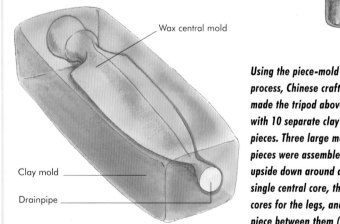

Wax central mold

Clay mold

Drainpipe

The lost-wax method of casting required only one mold, which a craftsman produced by making a wax model of the desired object, encasing it in clay, and firing the combined mold in an oven. The heat of the oven melted the wax, leaving a space into which the metal was poured.

Using the piece-mold process, Chinese craftsmen made the tripod above with 10 separate clay pieces. Three large mold pieces were assembled upside down around a single central core, three cores for the legs, and a piece between them (right). The cores and mold pieces formed a single mold into which molten bronze was poured. A base and lid prevented the molten bronze from flowing out.

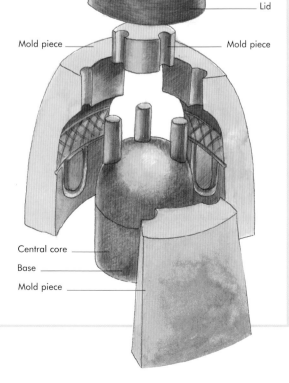

Lid

Mold piece

Mold piece

Central core

Base

Mold piece

Music that was played in the wrong tones could cause cosmic and social disruption. Unlike stringed instruments, bells do not go out of tune, so they set the standard within an orchestra. It was therefore of the utmost cosmic and political importance that the bronze-casters tuned each individual bell to maintain consistency within and between the sets of bells. Early Chinese bells gave only one musical note when struck. However, the inscriptions on the bells in Marquis Yi's tomb indicated that these late Zhou bells were designed to produce two notes. One note was obtained by striking the lower central part of the bell, the other by striking its side.

Scholars do not know exactly how the Zhou bronze-casters calculated the proportions of the bells in a set. When casting a single-toned bell, inconsistencies in pitch could to some extent be corrected by polishing or tempering (reheating and cooling) the bell. However, tuning two-toned bells was a delicate affair, because modifications to one tone affected the other. There was no easy technological fix: making these bell sets required considerable labor from skilled and experienced craftsmen.

Mass production

The Shang method of casting bronze developed out of pottery-making techniques. Potters in late Neolithic China had developed fine clay mixes and high-temperature firing techniques. These methods allowed them to produce elaborate decorative designs that retained their sharp outlines after firing. The same techniques were used to achieve the delicate and complex geometrical patterns characteristic of Shang and Zhou bronzes.

Potters also produced complex types of pots by making several parts separately and then neatly fitting them together before the final firing, a method known as modular production. The molds for bronzes were made through an extension of this process: a single shape was first disassembled into components, then reassembled so it could be cast in a single piece (see box on facing page).

Making modular pottery in this way was a complicated process: it required abstract thought, planning, standardization of parts, specialized division of labor, and probably the presence of a supervisor to coordinate the work and control quality. The necessity of making separate parts that match and fit together tends to restrict originality and variation in design, but modular production is fast, since several people are working simultaneously on the same object. The methods used to make these pots constitute a first step toward mass production, which emerged in its fully fledged form in late Zhou and early imperial China.

Shang workshops

Part of the Shang capital city at Anyang was occupied by a number of industrial workshops. Each workshop specialized in a particular material—jade and stone, bone, pottery, or bronze. The craftworkers lived nearby in small pit-houses. Archaeologists who excavated one workshop site found several hundred bronze-casting molds and many crucibles for heating the metal. Two to three hundred craftsmen must have worked together to produce some of the largest pieces. This scale of bronze production required control of ample supplies of valuable resources—including ores, clay, and fuel—as well as the authority and organizational ability to command the labor of large numbers of workers. In early China only rulers had the resources to run bronze foundries, and lesser aristocrats had to rely on gifts, exchanges, or warfare for their supplies of ritual vessels.

As a result of the development of modular production, a clear division of labor developed in China between experts and generalists. Unlike

Shang and Zhou workshops produced countless bronze vessels for ritual purposes. Decoration consisted of geometric or spiral motifs and imaginary beasts, such as the *taotie* monster mask on this Shang vessel.

19

the master craftsmen of medieval Europe who learned to practice every step of their craft (see Volume 3: Medieval Europe, page 20), Shang craftsmen were experts in one or two standardized steps in the process. The overall supervisor, a generalist, was a manager of labor and resources. He was not personally skilled in the technology, but he did need a general understanding of all the processes involved, and he had to be able to read and write.

In the 6th century BCE, craftsmen began to use ready-made clay pattern blocks to mold the decorations on their bronze pieces. Previously each mold had been individually fashioned, even where sets of several bronze vessels were made to a common design. Pattern blocks opened up the way for the mass production of bronzes. They also offered a type of mechanical reproduction that allowed for great stylistic variation. A skilled artist was needed to make the initial pattern blocks, but no special artistry was needed to use this pattern to add decorations to the basic mold. Artists were thus freed to develop different designs.

The foundry at Houma in modern Shanxi province, the site of the Jin state capital from 585 to 453 BCE, turned out huge numbers of bronzes. Some objects were of fine quality, but others were much poorer. Unlike earlier foundries, which did not offer goods for general sale, the lower-quality Houma bronzes seem to have been available to anyone. This development is evidence that the feudal system was falling apart during the Warring States era (480–221 BCE). The regulations that had restricted luxury goods to aristocrats were no longer observed. Merchants and scholars were now admitted to the ranks of government advisers. More goods and money were circulating, and rather than rank conferring wealth, wealth began to confer rank.

WARFARE

Shang dynasty rulers were able to send armies of up to 13,000 men into battle. Foot soldiers, armed with spears or bows and arrows, made up the bulk of the army. Squadrons of nobles in chariots, each man armed with a bronze halberd (a combination ax and spear mounted on a long wooden shaft), rode at the head of the foot soldiers and led the charge against the enemy. This type of warfare was still being practiced in the Spring and Autumn period (770–481 BCE) .

The size of armies increased dramatically during the Warring States period. The population had grown, thanks to improvements in farming technology, and many small states had been swallowed up by larger states, leaving these large states as contenders for power. These factors, together with new forms of military organization and advances in the design and production of weaponry, meant that commanders could now muster armies of several hundred thousand foot soldiers organized into units of crossbow archers, spearmen, and swordsmen.

The foot soldiers were disciplined and well drilled. They wore leather armor strengthened with lacquer (see page 25), and wielded well-made, mass-produced metal weapons. The crossbow and the sword were introduced, probably in the 4th century BCE, and cavalry began to replace the chariot, which had limited use on rough terrain. Commanders still rode in chariots, but the foot soldiers now led the charge against the enemy. Now commanders were organizers as much as warriors: with armies of such size, ensuring adequate supplies of food and spare weapons was no less important than coordinating troop movements.

Nothing was gained by utterly destroying the enemy's army and laying waste to its territories. Successful states increased their power and wealth by absorbing vanquished states into their own territory with as little physical damage as possible. Diplomatic negotiations and the humane treatment of beaten foes were as important in building a power base as winning battles. The state of Qin, in the northwest of China, emerged from the Warring States period as the strongest power in China. It had become wealthy through a combination of advanced farming methods and efficient taxation. Qin

Dunhuang

QILI
MTS
Wu-su

The state of Qin, located in the northwest of China, conquered the other Warring States by 221 BCE, and the Qin king Zheng took the name of Shihuangdi (First Emperor) of China. The Xiongnu, nomadic horsemen who lived to the north, frequently invaded China at this time. To halt their incursions Shihuangdi built a continuous earthern border along the northern frontier, the beginning of the Great Wall of China. The succeeding Han dynasty undertook military campaigns that expanded the empire's borders.

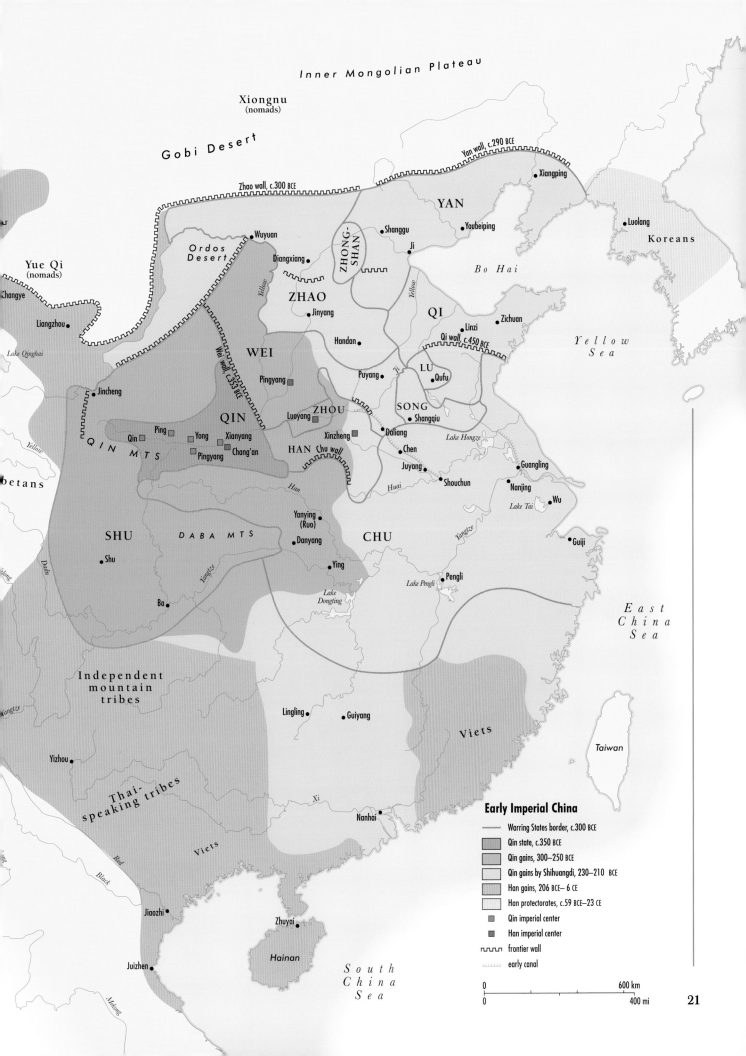

Inner Mongolian Plateau

Xiongnu
(nomads)

Gobi Desert

Zhao wall, c.300 BCE

Yan wall, c.290 BCE

• Xiangping

YAN

• Wuyuan

Ordos
Desert

• Diangxiang

ZHONG-
SHAN

• Shanggu

• Youbeiping

• Luolang

Koreans

Yue Qi
(nomads)

• Changye

• Liangzhou

Lake Qinghai

Yellow

ZHAO

• Jinyang

Ji

Bo Hai

• Handan

QI

• Linzi

• Zichuan

Yellow

Yellow
Sea

Qi wall, c.450 BCE

WEI

• Pingyang

• Puyang

Ji

LU

• Qufu

• Jincheng

Wei wall, c.353 BCE

QIN

Luoyang•

ZHOU

• Xinzheng

SONG

• Shangqiu

• Daliang

Tibetans

QIN MTS

• Qin

• Ping

• Yong

• Xianyang

• Chang'an

• Pingyang

HAN

Chu wall

• Chen

Lake Hongze

• Juyang

• Guangling

Yellow

Han

• Shouchun

• Nanjing

Huai

Lake Tai

• Wu

SHU

DABA MTS

Yanying
(Ruo)•

• Danyang

CHU

Yangtze

• Guiji

• Shu

• Ying

Lake Pengli

• Pengli

East
China
Sea

Dadu

• Ba

Lake
Dongting

Yangtze

Independent
mountain
tribes

Yangtze

• Lingling

• Guiyang

Viets

Taiwan

• Yizhou

Thai-
speaking
tribes

Xi

Viets

• Nanhai

Red

Black

• Jiaozhi

• Zhuyai

Hainan

South
China
Sea

• Juizhen

Mekong

Early Imperial China

⎯⎯⎯ Warring States border, c.300 BCE

Qin state, c.350 BCE

Qin gains, 300–250 BCE

Qin gains by Shihuangdi, 230–210 BCE

Han gains, 206 BCE– 6 CE

Han protectorates, c.59 BCE–23 CE

▪ Qin imperial center

▪ Han imperial center

⌐⌐⌐⌐ frontier wall

······ early canal

0 _____ 600 km
0 _____ 400 mi

⊗ THE CROSSBOW

A key factor in the state of Qin's military success was its use of advanced weaponry, particularly the crossbow. The crossbow consisted of a short bow fixed at right angles across the stock (a wooden support), which the archer held to his shoulder. He pulled back the bowstring and fired the bolt (a missile) by releasing the trigger. Crossbows were apparently invented in the southern state of Chu and were quickly adopted by neighboring states. Histories of the period tell us that in 209 BCE the second Qin emperor had 50,000 crossbow archers in his regiments.

Because the tension exerted on a crossbow's bowstring is much greater than that of a conventional bow, the bolt traveled farther and penetrated thick armor with ease. The spring-loaded trigger also gave the crossbow great accuracy over a long range. Solid ranks of crossbowmen opened battle by launching devastating assaults against the massed troops of an opposing army. Crossbows also proved effective weapons against the mounted troops of the Xiongnu and other nomadic marauders who frequently invaded China's northern borders.

The Han dynasty, which succeeded the Qin in 202 BCE, extended China's boundaries westward into Central Asia. Crossbowmen played a key role in the Han military campaigns. Early Han emperors banned the export of crossbow triggers and carried out searches of travelers at customs posts. But inevitably the ban was circumvented and the crossbow soon spread to neighboring regions, eventually reaching western Asia. Crossbows were known to the Romans, but did not become widely used in western Europe until the 11th century CE.

Crossbows are slower to load and to rearm than ordinary bows, making crossbowmen easy prey for an opposing army's advancing cavalry. To counter the problem, Chinese generals positioned crossbowmen next to archers armed with ordinary bows and soldiers with halberds. As the foe's cavalry approached, the crossbowmen fired their bolts, leaving the soldiers and quick-firing archers to shield them from attack while they rearmed.

Technical innovations steadily improved the crossbow. The addition of a foot loop (see top picture, below) made it easier for the crossbowman to exert pressure to draw back the bowstring. By the 2nd century BCE Chinese armies were using multiple-bolt crossbows, mounted on carriages, which used ox-power to draw back the bowstring. Later, sighting devices were added to enable more accurate aiming.

The basic trigger mechanism had already reached such perfection under the Han dynasty that minimal modifications were made to it in later times. The trigger, a fine example of standardized engineering, was a precision-built instrument made up of several bronze components (see picture, below). Standardization of production meant that any damaged trigger component could be easily replaced, even on the battlefield. Bolts were usually made of iron or of an iron-bronze alloy, tipped with bronze, in dimensions that fit exactly into the standard groove incised into the crossbow stock.

The crossbow was the rifle of its day, a lightweight weapon capable of firing accurately and repeatedly over long range. Its effectiveness depended on a high-grade trigger mechanism. The 6th-century BCE mechanism below consists of six bronze parts accurate to within fractions of a millimeter. Once assembled, the trigger looked very much like a modern rifle trigger (see the Warring States crossbow, bottom).

officials were noted for their honesty and loyalty, and the armies of Qin were renowned for their outstanding training and discipline. Qin craftsmen perfected the crossbow (see box on facing page), which was used in battle to devastating effect and gave Qin armies a great advantage over their opponents.

IRON PRODUCTION

Iron was first made in China in the 4th century BCE, nearly 1,000 years later than in the Near East. There was one very important difference between Western and Chinese ironmaking technology. From the start, the Chinese cast iron—they melted iron ore to liquid form in a furnace, and cast it into molds. In the Near East, iron was made by the bloomery or wrought-iron method, in which the iron is heated until it is soft enough to be hammered and bent into shape. This is called forging (see Volume 2: The Ancient Mediterranean, pages 45–47). Another difference was that Chinese iron production was done on a large scale, often in state-run workshops. By contrast, ironworkers in the West usually worked on their own, and their furnaces were much smaller. People in the Mediterranean and Europe did not begin casting iron (which requires much higher temperatures than wrought iron) until the 14th century CE.

Ironmaking appears to have developed in southern China as a by-product of bronze casting. When bronze is smelted on a large scale, small amounts of liquid iron are a natural waste product. Metalworkers would have found experimentally that it was possible to cast this liquid iron. In southern China, people used bronze not only for ritual vessels and aristocratic weapons but also for farm tools, including sickles and hoe-heads. Cast iron is hard and brittle, but it has the advantage of being cheaper than bronze, so metalworkers began to make farm tools of iron. Soon the Qin and other northern states were mass-producing iron as well. By about 300 BCE, iron pots and farm tools were common necessities for the peasantry. In warfare, iron

weapons replaced bronze in the 3rd or 4th century BCE.

Key to the Chinese ironmaking process was the blast furnace, which was fueled by charcoal. A current of air is forced at high pressure into the bottom of a blast furnace to create the very high temperatures needed to melt iron. At first, the Han used hand-operated box-bellows for this purpose. These bellows produced a blast of air on both the forward and backward stroke. Later they used waterwheels to operate the bellows. The movement of the water turned the wheel, which was connected to the machinery that opened and closed the bellows, forcing strong blasts of air into the furnace. Waterwheels were also used to drive sets of trip-hammers that broke up the iron ore.

Iron contains small amounts of carbon; carbon from the charcoal used as fuel mixes with the melted iron ore in the blast furnace. Chinese blast furnaces produced blocks of iron ("pigs") with a high carbon content of about 4 percent. After smelting, this pig-iron was melted again in another furnace and poured into molds to make cast-iron implements. Unlike early bronze casting, in which many vessels were made but each vessel was individually cast, the production of cast-iron goods usually involved the use of multiple molds so that several or even dozens of identical objects were made by each pouring of molten metal.

High-carbon iron is very hard and suitable for casting. But it is brittle and cannot be bent or shaped by hammering once it has solidified. Chinese ironworkers learned that if they kept the molten iron at 1600–1800°F (900–1000°C) for

Chinese metalworkers used these two halves of a mold to cast iron ax heads during the 5th century BCE. Using a large number of identical molds, iron-workers mass-produced iron tools and weapons in large workshops.

a day or two before casting it, the iron could be worked much more easily. This is because the carbon in molten iron combines with oxygen and is given off as gas. Iron produced in this way is called "malleable cast iron." Objects cast from malleable iron, such as plowshares, can be sharpened and re-sharpened by a blacksmith.

Han iron- and steelworking

In the early days of iron production under the Qin dynasty, ironworks seem to have been run by entrepreneurs who set up large camps in the mountains, close to deposits of iron ore and supplies of timber. However, in the 1st century BCE the Han state took direct control of iron production, appointing officials to run imperial foundries. There were some 50 "iron offices," whose blast furnaces were set up on the edges of cities, making and distributing iron goods.

Pig-iron from the blast furnaces was distributed to village smiths, who used it to make wrought iron. Wrought iron can be worked to produce a sharp edge, so it was used to make items such as knives. To make wrought iron, the smiths broke up the pig-iron and heated it to reduce its carbon content to about 0.1 percent (this is called fining). To make steel—which is both flexible and hard, and therefore ideal for such objects as swords—the smiths heated the wrought iron with charcoal to raise the carbon content again, to about 0.5–1.0 percent. The forging techniques of Chinese smiths included quench-hardening (plunging the hot steel into cold water) and "hundredfold refined steel." This process appears to have involved the smith repeatedly folding and welding a core of steel between two steels of different carbon content. It produced high-quality swords and sabers.

LUXURY GOODS

Weapons and everyday objects were not the only items that were mass-produced in early China. Imperial factories turned out huge quantities of luxury goods—lacquerware, silks, and ornamental bronzes—for emperors, princes, and high officials. Under the Qin and Han dynasties, commerce flourished. Political unification brought peace,

Production-line techniques turned out beautifully crafted lacquerware, such as this container, water pourer, and game box from the Han dynasty. Lacquerware was functional as well as decorative—its heat- and water-resistant qualities made it ideal for food vessels.

prosperity, and good transportation networks, which supported the growth of trade. A new class of bureaucrats arose when emperors established an imperial bureaucracy to manage the day-to-day affairs of the state. These well-paid bureaucrats needed fine fabrics and fancy serving dishes to perform their official duties, and purchased still more to satisfy their cravings for a luxurious private lifestyle. Luxury goods were also used as gifts to secure the loyalty of neighboring states and tribes.

Both imperial and private factories produced luxury goods, but the imperial workshops generally made the goods of highest quality and most elegant design. These state factories employed both men and women, and members of the same family followed the same craft for generations. Workers also included specialists drafted in from commercial workshops for two or three years of public service, or commoners performing labor service for the state. The skills and technical knowledge perfected in the imperial workshops were passed on to the commercial sector as workers returned to their former places of employment.

Commercial factories making lacquer, silks, and ornamental bronzes sprang up in the cities that were the seats of government. Factory owners often stamped their wares with inscriptions claiming that they were made in imperial workshops. However, there was usually no mistaking the difference in quality.

Lacquerware

Ritual feasts continued to be as important during the Han dynasty as they had been in Shang and Zhou times. But the Han ruling class preferred to use sets of elegant red-and-black dishes made from lacquer rather than the bronze vessels used by their predecessors. Lacquer is sap collected from a native Chinese tree, *Rhus vernifica*. The Chinese used it for making and decorating articles. During Han times, craftsmen dyed the lacquer red and black using cinnabar (a red mineral) and soot. They then applied the colored lacquer in layers (perhaps as many 20 or 30) to a base made of wood or molded hemp. Each layer took several days to dry and harden. When this stage of the process was complete, other craftsmen painted a design and applied a final layer of clear lacquer after the paint had dried. They sometimes added bronze fittings. Then the polishers went to work, giving the lacquer a hard and shiny surface. Finally, officials inspected the piece for quality and stamped it.

The manufacture of lacquerware was well suited to modular mass production because it involved multiple steps. In the Han imperial lacquer factories, small groups of specialists were assigned to each stage of production and the name of the leader of each group was stamped on the piece when it was completed. An inscription on the lid of a wine beaker dated to 4 BCE, for example, names five craftsmen involved in different stages of the beaker's production as well as the quality controller and chief foreman, and five levels of administrator. An inscription on one lacquer basin shows that it was number 1,450 out of a set of 5,000 made in 9 CE for an imperial palace.

Silk

Silk cloth was another commodity highly valued by the Chinese of the Qin and Han periods. The caterpillar of the silkworm moth, *Bombyx mori*, produces silk filament to build a cocoon in which it matures into the adult form. The cultivation of silkworms for silk production is called sericulture. It was practiced in China from at least 2000 BCE.

The silkworm's cocoon is made up of one continuous silk filament 2,000 to 3,000 feet (600 to 900 m) in length. To obtain the filament, workers first immersed cocoons in boiling water to kill the silkworms before the new moths broke through and tore the silk. They then unwound the filaments from several cocoons at the same time and twisted them together to make a yarn. About 2,000 cocoons are needed to produce just 1 pound (0.5 kg) of silk yarn.

Fine silk cloths were often painted with elaborate designs. This silk banner from the tomb of a Han noblewoman depicts the heavenly world, the human world, and the underworld. Dragons and other mythical beasts intertwine between the real and imaginary worlds.

In Han times, peasant farmers produced silk at home and wove plain silk on simple looms that produced a simple over-and-under (tabby) weave. The peasants gave most of what they made to the state as taxes. Government officials were then paid part of their salaries in the form of these plain silks, together with quantities of grain. They used the silks for clothing, as a writing medium, and also as a form of currency.

The royal family, court officials, and high-born women wore silks of a much higher quality. These robes were elaborately patterned with flowing motifs of phoenixes, grapes, or dragons. Silk weavers might take several months to weave a single piece of this type. The most sophisticated silks were produced in government factories, but private silk workshops also flourished.

The complex patterns of the best silks were made possible by the draw loom which used dozens of heddles—movable rods that deflected the warp (the vertical foundation threads) to either side. The draw loom's origins are uncertain—the Persians may have invented it—but it was certainly in use in China by Han times.

Like lacquerware, precious silks were an important diplomatic commodity, presented in large quantities to win the friendship of threatening tribes or allied states. Some of these fabrics ended up as far away as Rome. In Han times, the trade route known as the Silk Road stretched from China through central Asia to the eastern provinces of the Roman empire, from where precious goods, especially silk, were exported to Rome itself. It is often said that the Chinese tried to prevent the export of silkworms, but it is hard to see how they could halt the passage of such tiny items. By early medieval times, the oasis towns of central Asia produced high-quality silks.

TECHNOLOGIES OF IMMORTALITY

The ruling classes of early China devoted a great deal of time, ingenuity, and resources to preparations for the afterlife. The correct funerary practices, rulers and nobles believed,

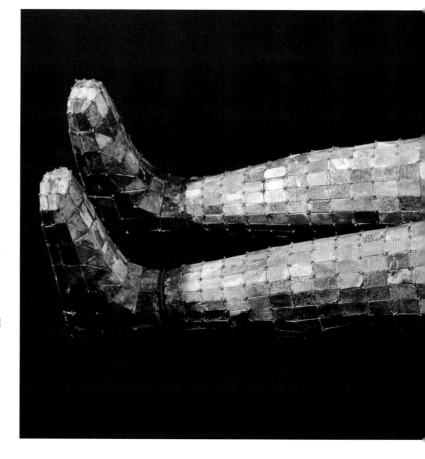

would ensure a pleasant existence after death. Shang and Zhou aristocrats were buried in tombs containing precious goods and human sacrifices that symbolized their high status in life. By the Warring States period, burial practices had changed, seeming to indicate a change in ideas about the afterlife. Personal belongings such as books and clothes were put in the tomb, as well as food, drink, and medicines.

Tombs were no longer just graves, but were constructed to resemble real dwellings. For example, Marquis Yi of Zeng's tomb, which dates from around 433 BCE, resembled a palace. It contained a bedchamber, armory, and ritual chamber, each furnished and decorated not just with ritual vessels but with all the artifacts, companions, and servants needed in everyday life. Some of these things were real, some were shown in pictures, and some were models.

By the Han dynasty, some two centuries later, tombs were decorated with murals or carvings showing scenes of upper-class and peasant life, and with pottery models of manors, rice fields and granaries, musicians and acrobats,

Aristocratic Chinese believed that certain substances, particularly jade, could assure them of life after death. The corpse of Princess Dou Wan, who died in the late 2nd century BCE, was encased from head to foot in a suit made from nearly 3,000 pieces of jade held together with gold wire.

horses drawing canopied chariots, and elegantly dressed servants. Corpses were embalmed to ensure that the dead person would awaken intact in the afterlife. The tomb of Lady Dai, who was buried at Mawangdui in modern Hunan province around 168 BCE, contained numerous texts on techniques for prolonging life. Archaeologists found traces of lead, mercury, cinnabar, and arsenic in her superbly preserved body. It is clear she had been eating these substances for some time before her death in the belief that they would give her immortality in the afterlife. Her clothes had been soaked in cinnabar, whose bright red color was associated with vital energy.

Jade was highly valued in China for its supposed life-preserving qualities, among other things. High-ranking people were sometimes buried in suits of jade during the Han period.

CONSTRUCTION PROJECTS

By far the most spectacular burial of early imperial China is the enormous necropolis of Shihuangdi, the Qin ruler who conquered seven rival warring states and who united China in 221 BCE (see pages 28–29). Shihuangdi was ruthless in pursuit of his ambitions. He had no qualms about emptying the empire's coffers to build palaces and pleasure parks, as well as his final resting place, and conscripting armies of peasants to work on these and other public projects, such as roads and canals. He also showed no regard for human suffering– thousands of laborers died in the harsh conditions of the construction sites. Others were killed to preserve the secrets of their work: the emperor ordered that all the craftsmen who had worked on his grave should be buried alive in the tomb when it was sealed.

The tombs of rulers and nobles included everything needed for a luxurious afterlife, including pottery models representing the estates on which they had once lived. This multistory house or watchtower is from a Han tomb.

Continues on page 30 **27**

THE TERRACOTTA ARMY OF SHIHUANGDI

Shihuangdi, the First Emperor of China, was obsessed by immortality. He died in 210 BCE, but preparations for his life in the underworld had begun much earlier. The Han historian Sima Qian, writing in the 1st century BCE, recorded that the future emperor put his chancellor in charge of planning and constructing his tomb as soon as he ascended the throne of Qin, at the age of 13, in 247 BCE. In 231 BCE, his chancellor chose the site of Liyi (near modern Xi'an in Shaanxi province) for the king's tomb and also for his palace. He instructed the inhabitants of the region, which was made a special administrative district, to begin constructing the two royal projects.

Once the king of Qin became emperor of China in 221 BCE, the project grew in scope. An additional 30,000 families were settled in Liyi, and conscript laborers, prisoners, and slaves were also brought in, so that some 700,000 people were working on the tomb by the time of the emperor's death in 210 BCE. The burial mound or mausoleum was a square-based, stepped pyramid of pounded earth, about 380 feet (115 m) high and 1,150 feet (350 m) wide. Grave robbers have raided parts of the mausoleum many times over the centuries, but most of it still remains unexcavated.

Shihuangdi's tomb appears to have been intended not only as a form of immortality for himself, but as a perpetuation of the dynasty that he had founded, and of the cosmos over which he reigned as the Son of Heaven. Under the burial chamber, Sima Qian tells us, "All the country's streams, the Yellow River and the Yangtze were reproduced in quicksilver [mercury] and by some mechanical means made to flow into a miniature ocean. The heavenly constellations were shown above, and the regions of the earth below."

In 1974 archaeologists were amazed to discover, not far from the burial mound, four huge pits containing an army of life-size statues of warriors and horses made from terracotta (unglazed fired clay). Nothing like this had ever been found before. Archaeologists have so far excavated and restored about 2,000 of the warriors. They estimate the army to number about 7,000 in total. The terracotta army includes infantrymen, archers, charioteers, and

The soldiers of the terracotta army are astonishingly lifelike—even the dressing of their hair is modeled in careful detail. No two figures are the same.

officers. The warriors carry bronze weapons; their clothing and armor, as well as their facial features, were made with great attention to detail. The figures were originally painted and lacquered to make them look even more realistic. Presumably this army was intended to serve as a magical force that would defend the dead emperor and his domains eternally against his enemies.

The terracotta figures provided scholars of Chinese technology with information about the way modular mass production was organized by the Qin state. Each of the figures was stamped or inscribed with dates, serial numbers, and the names of craftsmen. The names indicate that some of the craftsmen were originally makers of clay drainage pipes, who had installed the large-scale drainage systems that run under the Qin tomb and palaces. Their experience in making clay tubes was adapted to design the hollow arms, legs and torsos of the warriors.

Like Chinese pottery and bronzes, the terracotta figures were constructed in pieces. Each figure consisted of seven main parts: the base, feet, legs, torso, arms, hands, and head. Minor parts included eyebrows and moustaches, fingertips, and thumbs. The modelers assembled each figure before firing—joining the parts with strips of clay—and painted it afterward. The horses were made in a similar fashion. Although each part had only a few variants, the number of ways in which the parts could be put together was enormous. The obvious advantage of using this modular method of production was that the figures could be made much faster than if each had been individually designed. The total workforce of modelers appears to have been about 1,000, organized into small teams. The figures were apparently all completed and put in place between 221 and 210 BCE.

The terracotta soldiers were buried in pits standing in columns in regular military formations—ready to fight their master's enemies. The sheer size of the army testifies to Shihuangdi's power and concern with the afterlife and to the sophistication of the method of production.

The expense and brutality of the building program eventually led to the downfall of the Qin dynasty in 206 BCE, just four years after Shihuangdi's death. Built at massive financial and human cost, the Qin's monumental structures nevertheless clearly demonstrate the empire's advanced technologies and excellent organizational abilities.

The Great Wall

The best known of Shihuangdi's construction projects is the Great Wall. Between about 350 and 290 BCE several of the Warring States had built high walls of pounded earth, faced with brick or stone and studded with forts and lookout towers, to defend stretches of frontiers from attack by Xiongnu (Hun) warriors from the north. Shihuangdi put his general, Meng Tian, in charge of joining up these walls to make a continuous barrier along the northern frontier.

Between 221 and 210 BCE Meng Tian worked with a force of 300,000 soldiers, plus hundreds of thousands of conscript laborers. The completed wall stretched for more than 3,700 miles (6,000 km). It was up to 25 feet (7.5 m) tall. Over the centuries, it has been repaired, rebuilt, and extended continually and is an important tourist attraction today.

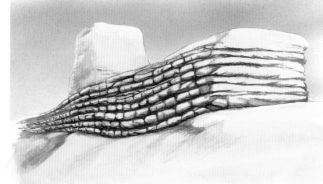

Workers built much of the original Great Wall using the rammed-earth technique (above). They tipped loose earth into a wooden frame and compacted it to a make a firm layer, repeating the process until the wall reached the desired height and the frame could be removed. Most of the present Great Wall (right) is the result of rebuilding in stone during the Ming dynasty (1368–1644).

Roads

Shihuangdi also built a network of post-roads, known as "straight roads" or "speedways," to connect distant provinces to his capital city, Xianyang (modern Xi'an). An essay addressed to a Han emperor around 178 BCE tells us that the highways built by Shihuangdi were broad and beautiful. They were about 50 feet (15 m) wide and planted with pine trees every 32 feet (10 m). Of the five main roads radiating from the capital, one went west into the Gobi Desert. Another, 950 miles (1,500 km) long, ran all the way to the Yangtze delta. The Qin built about 4,500 miles (7,000 km) of these roads altogether. The Han emperors added to the network, their most spectacular achievements being the carving of roads through mountain gorges into what are now the provinces of Sichuan (in the central west) and Yunnan (in the southwest).

The invention of the breaststrap harness in the 4th century BCE enabledo horses to pull heavier loads—a single horse wearing a breaststrap harness could haul about 1½ tons. Faster horse-drawn carriages replaced slow-moving ox carts for many purposes. Post-stations every 10 miles (15 km) along the empire's roads provided horses and carriages for official use. Officials riding in carriages traveled at around 9 mph (15 km/h). Horsemen bringing urgent news could get from Canton in southern China to the capital in less than a week. The main purpose of building the roads was to improve government efficiency but merchants also used the roads, and commerce expanded rapidly.

Irrigation and canals

Irrigation and flood control were constant preoccupations in many of China's fertile plains, and the Qin kings and emperors made lasting contributions to water engineering (hydraulics). One pioneering project was the Zhengguo Canal, which links two tributaries of the Yellow River in the region of Xianyang. The canal, completed in 246 BCE and still in use today, is about 95 miles (150 km) long and irrigates nearly 1,000 square miles (2,500 sq. km) of farmland. One story tells how the building of the canal grew out of the rivalries of the Warring States period. According to the story, the engineer Zheng Guo was sent to Qin by the king of Han, who hoped to trick Qin into exhausting its resources on this costly project. When the canal was well under way the king of Qin discovered the trick and confronted Zheng.

A bronze model of a covered chariot, one-third actual size, that was found buried near the terracotta army of the First Emperor. Each of the four horses wears a breaststrap harness attaching it to the chariot. Qin officials would have traveled in a fast-moving chariot like this.

Zheng argued that in the long run the canal would bring rich benefits to Qin; his life was spared and he was allowed to complete the project. The canal was indeed profitable. The Han historian Sima Qian tells us it transformed Qin into "a fertile country without bad years," making the state so rich and powerful that it was able to unite China.

In 316 BCE, Qin conquered the state of Shu, in modern Sichuan province. This was an important rice-growing area, and in 250 BCE the Shu governor, Li Bing, was ordered to construct an irrigation scheme at Dujiangyan, where the feeder streams of the upper Yangtze River tumble down from the Tibetan foothills into the fertile Chengdu plain. Here, Li Bing and his son Li Ergang built a system of canals that followed the contours of the hills to irrigate an area of land about 40 by 50 miles (65 by 80 km). Farmers still use the canals today, although they are now threatened by the Three Gorges Dam project.

Many parts of China were more easily accessible by river rather than by road, but travel between river valleys was often difficult. Probably the most innovative of all the Qin hydraulics works was the "Magic Canal." This was built by the military engineer Shi Lu in about 219 BCE, during the Qin's campaign to conquer the people of Yue along the southeastern coast. The genius of the canal, in a mountainous zone of modern Guangxi, is that it joins one river, the Xiang, which flows north to join the middle reaches of the Yangtze, to another, the Li, which flows south to join the West River and eventually reaches the sea at Canton. Shi built a canal through a pass in the mountains to join the two rivers close to their sources. The canal itself is only 3 miles (5 km) long and runs pretty much level, but to allow the smooth passage of transport ships from one river to the other, the engineer had to straighten out and deepen the channel of the Li River for a distance of 15 miles

These walls are all that remain of Jiaohe, a town established by the Han emperors in the far west of the country. A network of good roads linked even the most distant parts of China to the imperial capital.

(25 km). He built a series of spillways, evenly sloped shallow channels constructed parallel to the main river bed, to haul the boats up to the level of the canal. This piece of engineering, still used today, was the first to connect two of China's major river networks.

The other major Chinese transportation canal is the Grand Canal, which links the basins of the Yangtze and Yellow Rivers. The greatest part of this ambitious engineering work, which incorporated several stretches of canal built in Han times, was undertaken by Yangdi (reigned 604–617 CE), the second emperor of the Sui dynasty (581–618). The canal eventually extended 1,200 miles (1,900 km).

The end of early imperial rule

Construction projects under the Han were relatively modest in scale. The dynasty set its stamp upon Chinese history in other ways, creating a cultural pattern of respect for scholars, and for encouraging farming, as opposed to trade. The Han established institutions like the Imperial Library and the Imperial University, introduced the first examination system for civil servants, and commissioned scholars to edit the classic texts of philosophy, government, and medicine. And the Han emperors greatly expanded China, conquering large territories in the south, much of the Korean peninsula in the north, and part of central Asia to the west.

The cost of mounting military campaigns to defend its northern frontier against attacks by Xiongnu nomads gravely weakened the Han dynasty. A Han courtier, Wang Mang, led a rebellion that overthrew the Han in 9 CE. Though the Han took back the throne 14 years later, they were never able to reimpose a strong centralized state. The revenue-collecting system of the Han empire broke down, and rich landowners were able to increase their wealth and power. Peasant rebellions became common, and the Han emperors became more and more isolated from their subjects. In 220 CE, the last Han emperor was deposed, and the empire broke up into three separate kingdoms.

The Sui dynasty reunified China in 581 after more than three centuries of division and war. The Sui emperors, like the Qin emperors before them, undertook a series of ambitious nation-building construction schemes, including engineering projects of general benefit like roads, bridges, and canals, as well as luxuries for themselves, such as elaborate palaces and pleasure parks. All these projects absorbed huge amounts of materials and labor, and made heavy demands on the population. Like the First Emperor, Yangdi, the second Sui emperor (reigned 604–617 CE), was a much-hated figure, and his dynasty soon fell to the Tang dynasty (618–907). The Tang emperors presided over a golden cultural age. They extended China's borders farther than ever before into central Asia and Korea. But the gains proved difficult to hold against nomadic invasions, and internal rebellion further weakened Tang authority. In 907, the dynasty was overthrown and China broke up once again into nearly a dozen rival kingdoms.

Although the rebels who overthrew the Qin and Sui rulers did not hesitate to destroy their palaces and other monuments, they made full use of their great engineering projects to bring prosperity and administrative efficiency to their own regimes. The short-term costs of the grandiose projects of the Qin and Sui proved ruinous for the workers who built them, and for the rulers who pushed them through. But the long-term benefits were incalculable. As Zheng Guo said of his irrigation canal, "I am accomplishing a work that will sustain Qin for ten thousand generations." More than 2,000 years later, his canal is still watering the farmlands of northern China. And while the building of the Grand Canal contributed to the Sui dynasty's downfall, the canal itself became the economic backbone of China for the rest of the imperial era (see Volume 3: Late Imperial China).

The Grand Canal forms a north–south link between the Yangtze and Yellow Rivers, which flow mainly east–west. The canal is still vital to water transportation in eastern China, some 1,400 years after it was built.

THE ANCIENT MEDITERRANEAN

From about 3,500 years ago, the diverse peoples of the eastern Mediterranean came into contact with one another through trade, which brought great wealth, fostered new ideas, and led to advances in technology. On the island of Crete, the Minoan civilization, with its sophisticated craftworking techniques, rose and fell. Later, the Phoenicians dominated the Mediterranean, spreading their technological innovations throughout the region. The stage was set for the rise of the Classical Greeks and their remarkable advances in writing, science, and philosophy.

Around 1500 BCE, the lands that lie in an arc around the eastern end of the Mediterranean Sea contained many different societies, which varied considerably in terms of size, complexity, and technical sophistication. In the south lay Egypt, a stable, highly centralized state under the rule of the New Kingdom pharaohs (see Volume 1: Ancient Egypt). Traveling northeastward, the lands along the coast of present-day Israel and Syria (often referred to by ancient historians as the Levant, or the Near East) were occupied by many small city-states—independent states, based in a single city, that controlled a portion of the surrounding countryside. The peoples of the Levant at this time included the ancestors of

This simple pottery bowl comes from Akko (in present-day Israel), which was a Canaanite city-state in the 13th century BCE.

the Canaanites and Phoenicians, who are mentioned in the Bible.

To the north was the mountainous region of Anatolia (also called Asia Minor, what is today Turkey). At this time Anatolia was the center of a large kingdom inhabited by a people known as the Hittites. The Hittites' discovery of ironworking made them key figures in the history of technology (see pages 44–47).

Across from Asia Minor, on the other side of the Aegean Sea in what is now Greece, was

This 13th-century BCE Minoan fresco shows men rowing a ship from a harbor. Seaborne trade was crucial to the development of civilization in the Mediterranean.

3000 BCE	2500	2000	1500	1000

Development of cuneiform script in Mesopotamia

Tin is mined and smelted at what is now Goltepe, Turkey

Rise of the Minoan civilization on Crete

Minoan Linear A script comes into use

Mycenaean civilization emerges in southern mainland Greece

Ironworking emerges among the Hittites

Mycenaeans conquer Crete; Linear B script comes into use

The Sea Peoples invade Egypt and Near East; collapse Mycenaean and the Hittite empires; writing falls into disuse in Greece

1286 Traditional date of the Battle of Qadesh between Hittite and Egyptian armies

A cargo ship is wrecked off Ulu Burun, Turkey

Bronze Age   **'Dark Age'**

800	600	400	200

City-states emerge in mainland Greece and Asia Minor

Homer composes the *Iliad* and *Odyssey*

Black-figure style of vase painting flourishes in Athens

280 The *Pharos*, the greatest lighthouse of antiquity, built at Alexandria, Egypt

Greeks begin to colonize the Mediterranean and Black Seas

448 Greek city-states finally defeat a Persian invasion

334–324 Alexander the Great conquers Egypt and Persia, and campaigns as far as India

335 Aristotle founds a school of philosophy in Athens

Iron comes into widespread use in Greece; Phoenicians found trading colonies in the eastern Mediterranean

Phoenicians found Carthage (Tunis) as a trading capital; Greek alphabet comes into use

According to legend, the Phoenician fleet circumnavigates Africa, taking three years

447–432 The Parthenon temple is built in Athens

Plato founds the Academy, a school for philosophy

Classical Age

Hellenistic Age

Trade in the eastern Mediterranean

■ Bronze Age site
● Bronze Age shipwreck

areas with finds of foreign goods

▲ Canaanite amphora
▲ Mycenaean pottery
▲ Cypriot copper
▲ Cypriot pottery
△ glass from the Levant

— probable counterclockwise trade route of the Ulu Burun ship
— amber trading route

0 — 300 km
0 — 200 mi

another collection of kingdoms belonging to the Mycenaean civilization. The Mycenaeans were warriors who built citadels with large walls and buried their dead in deep shaft tombs. Outdoing them in technological skills, wealth, and influence were the Minoans, who, by about 2000 BCE, had established a civilization on the island of Crete at the southern end of the Aegean.

A HIGHWAY FOR TRADE

The Mediterranean Sea acted as a highway for trade, bringing the people who lived around its eastern shores and on its islands into close contact with each other. The powerful and wealthy rulers of these societies acted as patrons for specialist craftsmen, who produced valuable objects for ornamental or ritual use, as well as items such as stone or copper implements for everyday use. The raw materials needed to produce finished articles were not evenly distributed. One state might have access to sources of tin or gold, for example, so it would trade these materials with neighboring or more

distant states that needed them, acquiring in exchange some objects it lacked—items of jewelry, perhaps, or pottery vessels.

Egypt traded gold and semi-precious stones, and Egyptian traders also imported exotic materials such as ostrich eggs and ivory from tropical Africa along the Nile. Egypt imported lapis lazuli, a stone used in jewelry, from the Indian subcontinent via Mesopotamia, the region between the Euphrates and Tigris Rivers in present-day Iraq. Pack animals were used to carry some goods from India to Mesopotamia along overland routes. Trading vessels also brought goods by way of the Arabian Sea and Persian Gulf.

The Mycenaeans had access to honey, wax, and wood from the various farming peoples to the north of them in the Balkan peninsula and

Long-distance trade in the Late Bronze Age involved all the major powers of the eastern Mediterranean. The map shows the main towns and ports of the time. Archaeological discoveries of trade goods from foreign regions make it possible to trace long-distance trade routes.

around the Black Sea. The Mycenaeans were also at the southern end of the long-distance trade in amber—fossilized tree resin from the shores of the Baltic Sea in northern Europe. Orange in color, amber was used to make jewelry. Traders carried it along the rivers of Europe to the Mediterranean. Individual merchants did not travel the entire route; the amber passed through the hands of several middlemen along the way.

The Minoans traded obsidian, a naturally occurring shiny, black volcanic glass, found on Crete. There was also trade in glass ingots, which were made by the Egyptians and the peoples of the northern Levant by melting sand at a very high temperature and allowing it to harden. The ingots were re-melted to make beads.

Trading metals

One commodity held this trade system together—bronze, a mixture of copper and tin. Around 4200 BCE people in Mesopotamia learned to combine copper and tin by heating them together in a kiln. They also discovered how to cast bronze—heating the metal until it became a liquid and pouring it into molds. Bronze was used to make vessels and weapons, and by 3500 BCE bronze technology had spread throughout the eastern Mediterranean. (Bronzemaking technology is discussed more fully in the Early China chapter.)

Extensive trade routes grew up to supply copper and tin to those societies that knew how to use them. Sources of copper ore were scattered around the eastern Mediterranean: in Italy, the Balkans, Anatolia, the Sinai Desert between Egypt and the Near East, and the islands of Sardinia and Cyprus. Tin came from parts of central Europe, Anatolia, Spain, and as far away as India and England. The copper and tin ores passed from trader to trader in stages, in much the same way as amber.

Although archaeologists give the name Bronze Age to the period in western Asia and Europe between about 3500 and 1200 BCE, bronze was never that common in this period. Transportation of heavy ores, or even of metal ingots or finished metal

objects, was slow and difficult. Metal ores were often mined in remote mountainous regions and had to be carried over rough terrain to rivers, where they were loaded onto barges. Or they were shipped long distances across the sea.

Because the raw materials for bronze were hard to obtain and were traded over great distances, bronze objects were very highly valued. Local craftworkers manufactured bronze objects close to copper mines or at stops along the trade routes. As these bronze artifacts passed from a trader in one culture to a trader in another, they would acquire even higher value by virtue of their foreign origin. The fact that they were decorated with designs not locally available gave them added value.

The rich and powerful invested a great deal of time and energy in obtaining items made from bronze. Only rulers and their elite warriors had weapons and armor of bronze. Most everyday objects were made of other materials: agricultural tools from stone; cooking and storage vessels from pottery; clothes, including armor for ordinary soldiers, from wool and animal skins.

THE MINOANS AND MYCENAEANS

The hub of the Bronze Age trade network in the eastern Mediterranean was Crete, a rocky, mountainous island lying between Greece and north Africa. The ancient inhabitants of Crete are known as the Minoans. Crete lacked many

Networks of trade bound the various Bronze Age civilizations of the eastern Mediterranean loosely together. Minoan craftsmen in Crete probably used gold imported from Egypt to make this gold seal-ring for a Mycenaean warlord in Greece.

UNDERWATER ARCHAEOLOGY

How do archaeologists know what goods were being traded 3,500 years ago? Some of their information comes from the bottom of the sea. The Mediterranean Sea is notoriously treacherous for sailors. Dangerous currents swirl around its rocky coastline, and changes in the weather come rapidly and without warning. Before the invention of modern navigation and weather forecasting methods, ships were frequently lost at sea. The Mediterranean seabed is littered with shipwrecks from all periods of history.

Underwater archaeologists locate and excavate underwater sites using scuba gear and other special equipment, such as remote-controlled underwater cameras. In the 1980s archaeologists excavated an ancient shipwreck off a cape called Ulu Burun on the southwest coast of Turkey. Scientific dating methods showed that the ship had been built about 1300 BCE. Divers on the seabed uncovered all kinds of rare and valuable objects that allowed archaeologists to reconstruct the type of cargo carried by a coastal trading vessel of this period.

The mixed cargo included a ton of resin in two-handled jars, dozens of glass ingots, lumber, amber, tortoise shells, elephant tusks, hippopotamus teeth, ostrich eggs, olives in jars, and jars holding stacks of unused pottery vessels ready for sale. Archaeologists believe that the ship was on a counterclockwise trading trip around the eastern Mediterranean, buying and selling at ports down the line as it went. The lumber, amber, and olives were probably picked up in Mycenaean Greece, and the tusks, hippo teeth, and ostrich eggs (all from tropical Africa) in Egypt. The pottery and resin were from the southern Levant, and the glass ingots from farther north along the coast. The ship's next port of call would probably have been Anatolia, and much of the cargo may have been intended for a Hittite destination. But some of it may have been picked up for the next trip or to sell to a ship heading the other way; the resin was of a type that the Egyptians used in their mummification ceremonies (see Volume 1: Ancient Egypt, page 53).

As interesting as all these items were, the Ulu Burun wreck had still more significant information to give. The bulk of its cargo consisted of 200 copper ingots, each weighing 60 pounds (27 kg). These may have originally come from the island of Sardinia, in the western Mediterranean—confirmation of the extent and importance of the seagoing trade in metals.

The most common container for the transportation of goods was the two-handled Canaanite amphora. This one, raised from the Ulu Burun wreck, contained olives from Greece.

A diver examines part of the Ulu Burun wreck's cargo of 200 copper ingots.

resources, such as metal ores for metalworking and good clays for pottery-making, and the island was not flat or fertile enough to grow much wheat. The climate was good, however, for growing olives and grapes—which were made into olive oil and wine—and there was abundant obsidian. The Minoans, who were skillful sea-farers from early times, made up for their lack of resources by trading obsidian, olive oil, and wine with their mainland neighbors. By about 2000 BCE the Minoans had developed a complex civilization based on trade (see pages 42–43).

The island's rulers built huge palaces to display their wealth and power. Clay tablets found in these palaces are marked with a form of writing, which archaeologists call Linear A to distinguish it from the later Linear B script. Linear A appears to have been influenced by Egyptian hieroglyphics (pictorial script; see Volume 1: Ancient Egypt, pages 43–46). We cannot read these tablets because no one has yet been able to decipher Linear A. Archaeologists believe that Linear A tablets were inventories or lists of trade transactions, and it is probable that the Minoans developed writing to manage their commercial empire.

Archaeological evidence shows that beginning around 1600 BCE, a series of earthquakes and volcanic eruptions destroyed all the Minoan palaces. Some were partially rebuilt, but Minoan society seems never to have fully recovered from this devastation. The Minoan way of life finally ended in about 1450 BCE, probably because Crete was invaded by the Mycenaeans from mainland Greece, who were seeking to seize control of trade.

The Mycenaeans
The new rulers of Crete were much more warlike than the Minoans. At Mycenae in southern Greece, graves dating to between 1650 and 1550 BCE reveal evidence of a wealthy militaristic society. Stone reliefs show chariot-borne warriors armed with spears and swords.

From the 14th century, the Mycenaeans built palaces on mainland Greece that were strongly

This 4,000-year-old clay tablet from Crete is inscribed with a writing system known as Linear A. The Minoans probably used the script to keep track of their commercial interests. Linear A fell out of use around 1450 BCE with the coming of the Mycenaeans.

Continues on page 44 **41**

MINOAN TECHNOLOGY

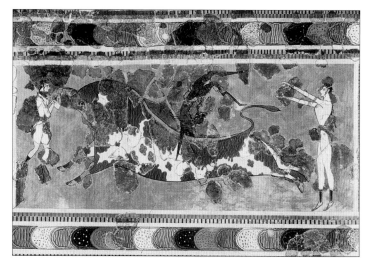

Trade was the driving force behind Minoan civilization and its technological activities. As trade increased, Minoan society became more complex and wealthy. By about 2000 BCE the Minoan world centered on four great palaces on Crete, at Knossos, Phaistos, Mallia, and Khania, which were probably the capitals of small kingdoms. Each palace was ruled by a king, who kept his people unified through elaborate religious rituals. These great palace complexes were centers for the collection and distribution of farm produce and trade goods, such as obsidian, which were brought there from surrounding areas along stone-paved roads. Imports, such as ingots of copper, were also stored at the palaces.

The largest palace, at Knossos, covered about 65,500 square feet (20,000 sq. m). Its multistoried buildings were laid out around a central courtyard and housed lavishly decorated state rooms, a number of grain and oil storerooms, workshops, shrines, and archives. The sophisticated sewerage and drainage system included stone slab-built sewage drains that were flushed by rainwater, and cisterns lined with waterproof plaster. Fresh water was delivered through a system of interlocking terracotta pipes, which were arranged so that the flow of water created a pressure that prevented the buildup of sediment.

The palace's foundations and lower levels were made of stone, the upper levels of mud brick, and the wooden roof

A fresco from the palace of Knossos shows athletes leaping over a bull's horns. Whether bull-leaping was part of a religious ritual or was merely a dangerous sport is unknown.

supports consisted of columns and crossbeams joined together by wooden pegs. Some archaeologists believe that these buildings may have been more resistant to earthquakes than the buildings of other Mediterranean peoples.

The wooden architectural elements were painted, and the interior walls covered with gypsum or plaster. Highly decorative frescoes showing religious rituals and scenes of palace life covered the walls of residential rooms and public areas.

The palaces were also centers of craft production; craftsmen manufactured a wide range of high-quality objects in palace workshops. Minoan pottery was particularly fine, ranging from a simple style suited to practical purposes—for example jars for transporting olive oil and wine—to much more elaborate types where the emphasis was on ornamentation. Excavation of a pottery workshop dating from around 2500 BCE—the oldest known from the Mediterranean—reveals that early Minoan potters made their wares on a flat disk which they turned by hand to produce round pots. The Minoans later pioneered the use of the potter's wheel turned by foot, developed a range of glazes and paints for decoration, and built sophisticated kilns for firing the pottery. As well as ceramics, Minoan artists produced spectacular objects of gold, silver, bronze, glass, and gemstone.

Minoan fleets dominated Mediterranean commerce until about 1430 BCE. Shipbuilders produced a range of boat types, including a 50-oar warship, the largest vessel of its day. The Minoans' navigational skills enabled them to establish colonies on nearby Aegean islands, and also as far away as Avaris on the Nile Delta.

The Minoans were expert potters whose products were in demand throughout the eastern Mediterranean. This elegant jug dates from 2000–1800 BCE.

Knossos was the largest of the Minoan palaces. Its ruins were excavated by British archaeologist Arthur Evans in the early 1900s. Evans rebuilt some of its fallen buildings. Visitors today can gain some idea of the palace at the height of its splendor 3,500 years ago, when its courts, shrines, storerooms, and workshops were crowded with people.

defended by walls of huge stone blocks. Each of these strongholds, under the rule of a king, controled the surrounding countryside and dominated sea trade routes. Mycenaean ships sailed throughout the eastern Mediterranean and as far west as Malta, Sicily, and the Italian peninsula in search of luxury goods.

After replacing the Minoans as the ruling power in Crete, the Mycenaeans created their own script partly based on Minoan Linear A. This is called Linear B. Scholars have deciphered Linear B, and from this they can tell that the Mycenaeans spoke a language similar to Greek.

The accomplishments of the Minoans and Mycenaeans led later Greek-speaking peoples to create legends about these civilizations. Mighty warriors must have built the the extensive fortifications of Mycenaean settlements, they said. According to Greek legend, a ruler of Crete, Minos, dominated the Aegean Sea with a huge fleet, and the technological know-how of the Minoans was the work of a genius named Daedalus. These stories—and perhaps memories of a sudden and devastating volcanic eruption or earthquake in the Aegean area—probably inspired the myth of Atlantis, an island civilization that ruled the world, and which, because of excessive pride, was destroyed by the gods in a tidal wave.

THE HITTITES

The Hittites, inhabitants of the mountainous region of central Anatolia, were at first minor players in the trade of the eastern Mediterranean. Originally farmers, the Hittites became militarily strong under a succession of kings in the 14th century BCE. They fortified their sacred capital of Hattusas (modern-day Bogazköy, Turkey), high in the Anatolian mountains, and began to conquer their neighbors to the south and east. They took control of important trading cities on

Carried by chariot and wielding a bow and arrow, a Hittite king crushes an enemy soldier in battle. The Hittites perfected the war chariot, which had been invented in the Near East around 3000 BCE, and used it widely.

the Levant coast of the Mediterranean where they clashed with the Egyptians, who were pushing into the region from the south. East of the Hittite kingdom was the Assyrian empire on the upper Tigris River in an area that encompassed parts of present-day Syria, Turkey, Iraq, and Iran. When the Hittites were not fighting the Assyrians, they were trading with them. The Hittites supplied the Assyrians with tin and lumber in exchange for luxury goods and materials such as lapis lazuli, which the Assyrians imported from India. The Hittites fed these items into the Mediterranean network through the trading cities they controlled on the coast.

Knowledge of ironworking

The Hittites owed at least part of their military success to a new technology–ironworking. Iron ore is one of the most common minerals on Earth. However, early attempts to smelt it in a kiln or furnace produced a dull, black metal that tarnished quickly into an unusable, crumbly mass. Lumps of this metal could be hammered to make small pieces of jewelry, but no matter how hard they tried, metalworkers of the Late Bronze Age could not melt iron in a furnace (that trick would not be learned for hundreds of years).

Iron in this unprocessed state, although harder than copper or tin, is softer than bronze. Iron therefore appeared of little use until, some-where in the Hittite empire, someone found that if small bits of iron were reheated at relatively low temperatures, without actually melting them, they could be hammered together (forged) to form a large piece. By trial and error, the Hittites found they could make many of these larger

This stone relief depicts a Hittite foot soldier marching into battle. Knowledge of ironworking allowed the Hittites to equip all their soldiers with metal weapons, not just an elite few.

The earliest recorded battle in history took place between the Hittites and Egyptians at Qadesh, Syria, in 1285 BCE. This illustration of an Egpytian sculpture commemorates the battle.

NOMADS OF THE STEPPES

Around 4000 BCE people living on the steppes (plains) of central Asia domesticated the horse. Initially horses would have been used as part of a mixed herding and farming economy in a similar way to sheep, goats, cattle, and other domesticated animals. But gradually farming began to diverge in two directions. In areas of good soils and manageable water supplies, such as Egypt and the Near East, crop cultivation became more important, and people began to live in permanent farming villages. However, on the steppes and in other regions where land was poor and irrigation not as manageable, seminomadic people (known as pastoralists) depended almost entirely on their herds for sustenance. Because grazing lands were quickly exhausted, they had to move their livestock frequently in search of new pastures. So their way of life became nomadic.

A further change came when these nomadic pastoralists learned to ride horses, instead of using them to pull carts. They were now able to drive their herds a far greater distance than before. They developed sophisticated technologies to go with their new lifestyle: they had well-made carts and wagons for transportation, and pioneered the use of woolen textiles and leather to produce clothing, tents, and other fixtures. Still, a mobile lifestyle meant that their wealth was mainly tied up in livestock, and they could not become technologically superior in activities such as metallurgy where a settled lifestyle is a big advantage.

Nomads relied on their settled neighbors to supply them with finished luxury goods and certain agricultural products like wine. In return, they supplied meat, wool, and dairy products to the villagers. Archaeologists think that one reason the nomadic lifestyle arose was that there were settled peoples capable of producing surplus goods. Because nomads were mobile, they were able to mix raiding and looting with peaceful trade. One of the most prominent of the pastoral nomadic groups in central Asia were the Scythians, who traded with the Greeks around the coast of the Black Sea in the 1st millennium BCE.

The Scythian nomads placed high value on gold items, which were easy to transport and conspicuously displayed their wealth. This gold comb, decorated with a scene of battle, dates from about 400 BCE.

pieces as hard or harder than bronze. Without knowing how or why the process worked, they discovered the trick of making steel by the direct method (see pages 48–49).

The ability to turn iron into steel increased the economic potential of iron. On the one hand, it took great practice and a good deal of work to produce iron, especially compared to bronze. Often the product was inferior and might have to be discarded because, unlike bronze, iron cannot be remelted and reused. On the other hand, the raw materials for iron were plentiful and cheap, while those for bronze were scarce and obtained through distant trade networks.

The Hittites were a warlike people, and they were soon producing iron weapons, armor, and chariot fittings. But their objects of value continued to be made of bronze, gold, and silver, and their everyday tools of stone. Their iron was not superior to well-made bronze, but it was just as good, and it enabled the Hittites to equip and field a very large army.

Around 1300 BCE the Hittites and Egyptians met in battle at Qadesh, in what is today Syria. The Egyptians, armed with traditional Bronze Age materials, fought the Hittites to a standstill, with both sides claiming victory. This outcome suggests that iron weapons, while important, were not an overwhelming military factor at this time. However, the Hittites went to great lengths to keep their iron-forging methods secret, so they must have put a high value on them.

END OF THE BRONZE AGE

Around 1200 BCE the Hittite empire collapsed. It is one among a number of disasters that appear in the archaeological record at this time. For example, the rulers of Egypt retreated to their former borders (see Volume 1: Ancient Egypt, page 62); Mycenaean citadels in Greece were burned and destroyed, and so were trading cities along the Levant coast. We can only guess at the causes of these events. However, changes

in pottery styles and other archaeological clues suggest there was great movement of peoples throughout the region at this time. These mass migrations may have been due to changes in climate or other natural factors. But it is probable that changes affecting the lives of nomads living on the fringes of the ancient civilizations of the eastern Mediterranean (see box at left) had a part to play in these events.

Comparatively small changes in climate, such as a prolonged drought, could cause these nomadic herders to alter substantially their usual seasonal migration patterns. As their pastures dried up, they would travel further in search of new ones and increase their raiding of nearby civilizations. If those civilizations were in a weak situation politically or militarily, perhaps even because of the same drought, then the nomads might actually be able to conquer them.

Whenever these nomads were on the move, they disrupted the peoples around them, which often had a domino effect on other peoples. This happened again and again through history. For instance, the movement of the Huns from central Asia into Europe in the 6th century CE set up a wave of migrations among the Germanic peoples who were settled on the edge of the Roman empire. This helped to bring about the empire's collapse and started the period of history known as the European Dark Ages. Historians believe that something similar took place at the end of the Late Bronze Age.

Experts have sometimes called this period "the First Dark Age" because the writing of Linear B fell out of use in Greece. Few records in cuneiform (see pages 54–55), the script that had been used throughout the Near East for more than 2,000 years, survive either. This suggests that the political stability to support large technical systems such as writing had disappeared. But although the larger centers of civilization fell, it does not mean that life was technologically inferior at this time in terms of knowledge or people's everyday lives. The age is "dark" simply because historians lack texts to cast light upon it.

Continues on page 50 **47**

SECRETS OF IRON AND STEEL

Iron has two big advantages over bronze, an alloy (mixture) of copper and tin. First, iron ore, a reddish-brown mineral, is much more common than copper or tin. Second, well-made iron is as strong as bronze, and steel (a mixture of iron and carbon) is stronger still. However, ironmaking involves much more complex technology than does bronzemaking, and it took several centuries of trial and error to perfect the correct ironmaking techniques.

Iron has a much higher melting point than copper or tin. When copper or tin ores are smelted (heated to high temperatures in a furnace) they form two liquids—the molten metal and a hot liquid (the slag) containing everything else. If iron is heated to the same temperatures, however, most of the slag melts and flows away, but the iron remains in what is called the "solid state." The higher temperatures required to reduce iron to a liquid for casting were not achieved in Europe for hundreds of years, though the Chinese were casting iron by the 4th century BCE (see Volume 2: Early China, pages 17–18).

Smelting iron ore in a furnace at low temperatures, as the peoples of the ancient Mediterranean did, produces a sponge-like lump known as the bloom. This is honeycombed with small holes and passages filled with slag that did not escape and solidifies as it cools. Reheating the bloom softens the trapped slag, which is then dislodged by hammering, leaving an iron ingot. This process is called forging and is done in a special fireplace called a forge.

Metalworkers in ancient civilizations would have observed that some forged (wrought) iron was harder than others. Trial and error would have taught them that the amount of charcoal used in the firing process affected the metal's hardness. Of course they would have had no idea that this is because of the presence of carbon in the fuel. When carbon combines with bloomery iron in the furnace or forge, the resultant mixture, steel, has some of the properties of an alloy. It is harder and can be worked to an edge by repeated heating and hammering. This technique is akin to annealing, which metalworkers already knew about from working with copper and bronze.

Early metalworkers made one more surprising discovery. Steel has a unique property—when reheated and quenched (that is, cooled rapidly by being dunked in water), it becomes even harder, much harder than any other metal known to the ancients. Ironworkers soon developed a large range of new techniques to take advantage of this discovery.

Ironworking took a lot of skill and hard work. Smelting and forging were separate tasks, using different techniques and knowledge, and forging required great manual dexterity and skill. Furthermore, the work was time-consuming and labor intensive. A new profession arose, that of ironsmith, and to learn the skills the smith took an extensive apprenticeship to master. A society that wanted to use iron had to be able to support a large number of specialized craftsmen. However, the pay-off was that the superior iron and steel tools and weapons were capable of generating even greater wealth

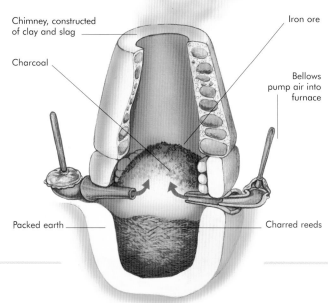

Chimney, constructed of clay and slag

Iron ore

Charcoal

Bellows pump air into furnace

Packed earth

Charred reeds

Early metalworkers smelted iron in a furnace consisting of a chimney built over a pit in the ground. The ore was placed on smoldering charcoal, and workers used hand bellows to force air into the furnace to raise the temperature.

Iron was at first traded
in such small quantities
that it rivaled gold as a
prestige material. One of two
ceremonial daggers placed inside
the tomb of the Egyptian pharaoh
Tutankhamun (d. 1323 BCE) has an iron
blade (left); the other is made of gold (right).
Both have golden scabbards. The iron dagger was
probably a gift to the king from the Hittites, who at
this time closely guarded the secrets of ironmaking. Only
after about 900 BCE did iron goods become abundant.

A temple relief shows the pharaoh Ramses II in battle against the Peoples of the Sea, who attacked Egypt at the end of the 13th century BCE. They were finally driven off by Ramses III after a decisive naval battle in 1180 BCE.

The Peoples of the Sea

One clue to what may have caused the First Dark Age comes from later Greek legends, which speak of waves of invaders from the north, first the Achaeans and then the Dorians. The Greek poet Homer composed his epics, *The Iliad* and *The Odyssey,* in the 8th century BCE, but the stories they tell of a war between the Greeks and the city of Troy in Anatolia probably refer to real events that took place some 400 years earlier.

In Egypt, inscriptions from this period describe a battle fought in the Nile Delta region, when the pharaoh's army defeated a large collection of tribes referred to simply as the "Peoples of the Sea." Archaeologists do not know just who these people were, but it seems likely that they included some of the invaders who had attacked sites in Greece and Anatolia, as well as some of the people they had displaced. Records show that the Egyptian army used mercenary troops from neighboring desert tribes and from Nubia, the region to the south, and some of these professional soldiers may also have taken the opportunity to turn on their former employers.

From their heartland in the Levant, the Phoenicians expanded westward, establishing a chain of colonies to carry out trade. Intermediary trading stations provided convenient ports of call for their vessels.

Some of the Peoples of the Sea may have remained in the area of the Aegean when the rest of their number went on to attack Egypt. Or they may have returned there after their defeat and settled on the Aegean islands as the ancestors of the people known as the Ionian Greeks. If that is so, then the Peoples of the Sea may have spoken Greek. But we cannot be sure of this because they left no written record.

Archaeologists believe that another group of Peoples of the Sea turned east from Egypt and settled along the southern Levant coast. They were the ancestors of the people known in the Bible as the Philistines, and they later gave their name to the region known historically as Palestine, which includes the modern-day nation of Israel. At around the same time, Semitic tribes settled west of the Jordan valley as the northern neighbors (and eventual enemies) of the Philistines. These people were the Hebrews (also known as the Israelites). The Bible suggests that they were slaves in Egypt. Their journey— or exodus—across the Sinai peninsula may have been due to the weakening of Egypt by the Peoples of the Sea.

The use of iron spreads

All these societies had ironmaking technology. So did the Greek-speaking peoples who began to form city-states in Greece, Crete, along the Anatolian coast, and on the Aegean islands some time after 900 BCE. And so did the emerging small kingdoms of the Italian peninsula that developed into the city-states of the Etruscans, and were later absorbed by the Romans.

It is not clear how knowledge of ironmaking spread. Perhaps as the Hittites declined, their ironsmiths traveled to other lands to find patrons. Perhaps foreign mercenaries in the Hittite army learned the secrets of iron during their stay in Anatolia and smuggled them abroad. Or perhaps Hittite iron objects obtained through trade or war spurred local inventors to experiment with the metal until they learned the secret themselves.

Because iron ore is so common compared to other metals, it could be used by almost any society, but only if that society had the political and social mechanisms to support a specialist workforce of ironworkers. These conditions existed among the city-states of the eastern Mediterranean, and so archaeologists and historians call the period from about 900 to 500 BCE the Early Iron Age.

THE PHOENICIANS

Trade all but ceased in the eastern Mediterranean during the First Dark Age. But it began to revive again around 1000 BCE, a sure sign that political stability and prosperity was beginning to return to the region. The people who led this trade were the Phoenicians, who lived in what is northern Israel and Lebanon today.

The Phoenician homeland was a narrow strip, only about 200 miles (320 km) long and 15 miles (25 km) wide, between the mountains of Lebanon and the Mediterranean. It was not rich in natural resources, but the Phoenicians had access to one invaluable

Glass pendants like this one were made in Phoenician workshops mainly for export. They have been found all over the Mediterranean, as well as in northern Europe and Russia—an indication of the extensive nature of Phoenician trade networks.

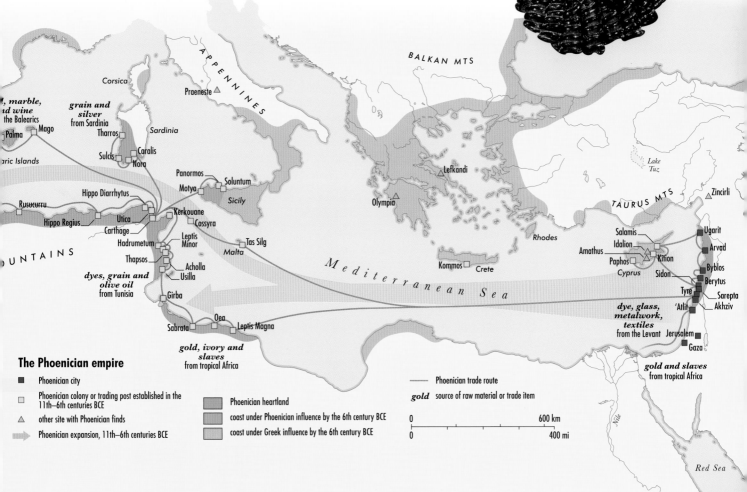

The Phoenician empire

- ■ Phoenician city
- □ Phoenician colony or trading post established in the 11th–6th centuries BCE
- △ other site with Phoenician finds
- ⇒ Phoenician expansion, 11th–6th centuries BCE

Phoenician heartland

coast under Phoenician influence by the 6th century BCE

coast under Greek influence by the 6th century BCE

— Phoenician trade route

gold source of raw material or trade item

0   600 km
0   400 mi

Both the Phoenicians and Greeks used the trireme, which had rowers sitting in three vertical tiers, one above the other. The Greek sculpture at top shows a single tier of rowers. The rowers could propel the trireme at great speed when there was no wind, or when the ship was close to shore, or in battle. The trireme's pointed bow, visible on the Phoenician coin (inset), was used as a ram to disable and sink enemy ships.

commodity—excellent lumber, particularly cedarwood, from the nearby mountain forests. Moreover, their coastal cities of Byblos, Tyre, and Sidon were ideally placed to control seaborne trade between the Assyrian empire, Egypt, and the rising city-states of the Aegean, Greece, and Italy. Soon Phoenician ships were sailing the coastal waters in great numbers, carrying larger and more diverse cargoes than even in Minoan and Mycenaean times.

Technological innovators

The Phoenicians were great technologists whose innovations would influence the history of the whole Mediterranean region, Europe, Asia, and, ultimately, the entire world. One of their areas of expertise was in shipbuilding. As well the trireme, a fighting ship powered by three tiers of oars, the Phoenicians built sea-going cargo ships.

Phoenician sailors developed navigational skills to the point that they ventured beyond the Mediterranean into the waters of the Atlantic Ocean. They explored the west coast of Africa and sailed to Cornwall, in southwest Britain, in search of tin. According to the Greek historian Herodotus (c. 485–c. 425 BCE), a Phoenician fleet set out from the Red Sea on the orders of the Egyptian pharaoh Necho to explore the east coast of Africa. The fleet is said to have rounded the Cape of Good Hope, and traveled up the west coast of Africa, reaching the Mediterranean about two years after it set out.

With few resources other than wood, the Phoenicians focused on being middlemen in trade transactions and also only manufacturing high-value finished goods from materials they imported from other countries. For example, they made finely carved ivory plaques from elephant tusks imported from Egypt for export. They also made and exported elaborately worked bowls and other vessels of bronze, gold, or silver.

Phoenician craftsmen also took advantage of materials closer to hand, such as sand, which they heated to make molded glass beads and pendants, using methods first developed by the Egyptians (see Volume 1: Ancient Egypt). Phoenician glassmakers added metallic oxides to color the glass. Phoenician textile workers discovered how to produce a unique purple dye from the ink of a local shellfish. Purple became the color of authority throughout the ancient world: for example, it was the color of the stripe on a Roman toga that denoted the rank of senator. The term Phoenician, first used in Greek texts of the 8th century BCE, means "purple-red."

As a result of their growing economic success, the Phoenicians established trading colonies on the islands of Rhodes, Cyprus, Sicily, and Sardinia; in southern Spain; and on the coast of north Africa. The Phoenician town of Carthage in north Africa was the largest city in the ancient world before the rise of Rome. It was to keep track of this vast trade and of their growing empire that the Phoenicians made perhaps their most important invention of all— the alphabet (see pages 54–55). The ability to easily record, preserve, and transfer information profoundly influenced the entire ancient world. If the Phoenicians had done nothing else, the invention of the alphabet would confirm their place in history. The scientific achievements of the Classical Greeks and the engineering feats of the Romans would not have been possible without it.

THE CLASSICAL GREEKS

Greece is a land of fertile valleys and coastal plains separated from each other by mountain ranges and rocky coastlines. It also has many islands scattered across the Aegean Sea. Although mainland Greece was rich in iron ore, lumber, and other resources, each valley could grow enough food to support only a limited population. This explains why, as Mediterranean trade revived in the early Iron Age, Greece developed into a network of independent city-states rather than a kingdom or empire under a single ruler. The city-states competed for trading advantage, and several sent groups of citizens overseas to found trading colonies. Most of these colonies were on islands and headlands along the coast of Anatolia (which the Greeks called Ionia). Some Greek colonies were founded around the Black Sea, and also to the west of Greece, in Sicily and southern Italy.

The Greeks grew olives for olive oil and grapes for wine. They imported foodstuffs from other parts of the Mediterranean. Greek farmers therefore participated in the trade network just as much as the artisans who produced decorated pottery and fine metalwork. Articles of Greek manufacture have been found in burials from the Black Sea to northern Germany, showing the great distances their goods traveled.

The Greeks at war

The Greek city-states had slaves, as did most other ancient societies, but only free citizens served as soldiers. The abundance of iron meant that every free adult male member of Greek society could be armed.

The Greeks were not as technologically innovative as the Phoenicians but they were extremely quick to pick up and improve on existing techniques. For example, the Greeks adopted the trireme from the Phoenicians. Wars were frequent between the rival city-states, and

Continues on page 56

A Greek foot soldier, or *hoplite*, wore light body armor. Although equipped with a sword, his most important weapon was a spear tipped with a fearsome point (below left). *Hoplites* fought in tight formations called phalanxes (bottom), which presented a wall of shields and a terrifying hedge of spears to the enemy.

THE ALPHABET

During the 3rd millennium BCE, a writing system based on cuneiform script evolved in the Near East. People enscribed the wedge-shaped symbols of this script by pressing a reed stylus onto clay tablets (see Volume 1: Ancient Egypt, pages 40–41). Cuneiform script mixed ideographs (picture symbols that represented a particular idea or thing) with syllabic marks that indicated the vowel sound of a syllable, which was determined by its context. This approach gave rise to an immense number of symbols. Late cuneiform had almost 1,000 signs, each of which could mean different things in different combinations. Even the relatively advanced and simplified Mycenaean Linear B script had 89 characters. Cuneiform—and its related scripts—was obviously a very cumbersome system to use. It took scribes many years to learn all the symbols. Literacy was the preserve of a tiny group of people.

Between 1500 and 1200 BCE, the Canaanites—the peoples of the Levant who were the ancestors of the Phoenicians—began to develop a simplified script based on a pared-down number of characters. They no longer used the ideographic aspect of the language, so the symbols did not need to resemble pictures. The Hebrew script of the Bible preserves this Canaanite system.

Then the Phoenicians realized that words can be broken down into a number of distinct sounds or phonemes (what we now call consonants and vowels). They decided that their symbols would represent its initial consonant sound—for example, "n" is the initial consonant of the symbol *nahs*, which was based on the original ideograph for "snake." The Phoenicians did not indicate vowels; readers simply guessed the vowels using their knowledge of the language.

Greek letters, such as these inscribed on part of a column, were "borrowed" from the Phoenician alphabet in about 800 BCE. The key Greek innovation was to add letters for the five vowels: a, e, i, o, u.

Each of the Phoenicians' symbols (they now numbered less than three dozen) had phonetic value only—it was what we would call a true letter. The first two letters of the Phoenician alphabet were *alef* and *bet*. The Greek alphabet, based on the Phoenician one, called these letters *alpha* and *beta*. Put together, they make up the word "alphabet"— any system of writing based on phonetic letters.

With the alphabet, a learner had only to master a handful of symbols, rather than several thousand, and could sound out written documents without special knowledge, only needing to know the phonetic values of the letters. Priests and scribes no longer had a monopoly on the written record. Individual merchants could keep track of their inventory, write contracts with partners, and even send letters to friends. Another advantage of the alphabet was that the simplified symbols could be written more rapidly than cuneiform script.

Because the Phoenician system of writing was so efficient, it quickly spread throughout the Mediterranean and Near Eastern trading networks. The Greeks added letters to indicate vowel sounds, making it even more flexible. The Etruscans of Italy adopted a form of the Greek alphabet, and introduced it to the small city-state of Rome. The Romans further refined it, and theirs is the alphabet that we use today in the west. The modern Persian and Indian scripts are also descended from the Phoenician alphabet.

Cuneiform script was used to write several Near Eastern languages, including Sumerian, Assyrian, Hittite, and Babylonian. The script on this tablet, bearing the impression of a royal seal, records the divorce decree of the Hittite ruler Mursil II (1345–20 BCE).

Our alphabet can be traced back to Proto-Canaanite script. Its signs were based on hieroglyphs but, instead of complete words, they stood for consonants. This system was developed further by the Phoenicians, who introduced their alphabet to the Greeks. They, in turn, improved it by using some letters to represent vowel sounds instead of consonants. The Romans' Latin alphabet was based on the Greek.

Proto Canaanite	Early letter names and meanings	Phoenician	Early Greek	Early monumental Latin	Modern English
	alp **oxhead**				A
	bêt **house**				B
	gaml **throwstick**				C
	digg **fish**				D
	hô(?) **man calling**				E
	wô **mace**				F
	zê(n) **?**				
	hê(t) **fence?**				H
	tê(t) **spindle?**				
	yad **arm**				I
	kapp **palm**				K
	lamd **ox-goad**				L
	mêm **water**				M
	nahs **snake**				N
	cên **eye**				O
	pi't **corner?**				P
	sa(d) **plant**				
	qu(p) **?**				Q
	ra's **head of man**				R
	taan **composite bow**				S
	tô **owner's mark**				T

55

fighting battles at sea required well-trained crews of oarsmen who could work together. The Greeks found that the same sort of teamwork paid off when fighting battles on land. Horse-drawn war chariots, used to great effect in Mesopotamia and the Near East, were worthless in the mountainous terrain of Greece. Instead, the Greeks trained land soldiers to march and fight together just as oarsmen rowed together.

The Greeks invented a military technique called the phalanx, in which foot soldiers armed with shields and spears of varying lengths fought in close formations that produced a wall of points (see picture on page 53). There was no place for individual heroics: a soldier could not fight effectively as a single unit and any action that threatened the integrity of the phalanx was frowned upon. The phalanx proved to be extremely effective in battle. When properly used, in relatively flat conditions, it could even defeat cavalry and chariots.

Rival city-states

How did the Greek city-states go about organizing a steady supply of citizen-soldiers for their armies and navies? Sparta and Athens, the two most successful and powerful states, took different approaches. Sparta militarized the entire population—boys were removed from their parents at age seven to be raised by the state and trained in self-discipline. At age 20 they became full citizens and joined a military unit. They were not allowed to set up their own household until age 30. Under the Spartan system, everyone was equal but subject to state control.

Athens took a very different approach, opting for greater democracy and individual rights. All Athenian citizens—freeborn males older than 20—served as soldiers and participated

The Athenians built the Parthenon in 447–438 BCE as a temple to their patron goddess, Athena. The building's great size and intricate decorations reflected the leading role Athens had assumed among the Greek city-states by this time. The ruins of the Parthenon still dominate the Athenian skyline today.

Greek pottery vessels and vases were painted with mythological stories rendered as detailed action scenes. This vase, made around 500 BCE, depicts an incident from Homer's epic poem, *The Odyssey*. Orestes murders his mother and her lover to avenge the death of his father, King Agamemnon, who led the Greeks in the Trojan war.

in decisions affecting the state, including declarations of war, through citizen committees and assemblies. In time, Athens became the most influential of the Greek city-states, thanks largely to its domination of Mediterranean trade, which it managed through its control over the Aegean and Ionian city-states.

The rivalry between the city-states, particularly Sparta and Athens, was temporarily halted when all were faced by a common enemy—the Persians. In the 6th century BCE, the Persian empire had become the most powerful military state in the Near East, replacing the Assyrians and Babylonians, and even extending its rule across present-day Iran as far as the Indus River. Persia had conquered the Levant, Egypt, and Anatolia, a feat never before achieved. When the conquered Greek city-states of Ionia rebelled against Persian rule, they called upon the mainland Greeks for help. The rebellion failed, and the Persians then set their sights on conquering

Greece. In a series of wars between 490 and 448 BCE, the Persians managed to sack Athens and some other Greek cities, but in the end their vast empire was defeated by an alliance of small Greek city-states headed by Sparta and Athens. A combination of resolve, better military tactics, and advanced technology—particularly their superior ships—brought the Greeks victory over a numerically much stronger enemy.

Art, science, and philosophy

As the Greek city-states grew wealthier from trade, a distinct Greek culture began to form. In art—especially sculpture and pottery—the Greeks were at first influenced by Egypt and the Near East, but the new naturalistic styles that emerged in the 7th and 6th centuries BCE laid the foundations of the later Classical Greek style. The Greeks learned sculpture from the Egyptians. At first they carved figures that were stiff and formal, but over time their sculpture became more graceful and naturalistic. Similarly, the geometric patterns that adorned early pottery gave way to scenes from myths painted in a naturalistic style (see picture on page 57).

Literacy spread rapidly after the Greeks adopted and refined the Phoenician alphabet. The Greeks used writing for practical purposes— to draw up law codes, record legal judgments, and transact trade. Writing also fueled a hugely creative literary culture. Homer composed his poems for public recitation in the 8th century BCE. They were not written down until long after his death. By the 6th century BCE the Greeks had invented drama and the theater. The tragedies of the Athenian playwrights Aeschylus (c. 525–465 BCE) and Sophocles (c. 496–405 BCE) are among the Classical Greek plays still performed today.

Wealth gave upper-class Greeks free time to devote to pursuits such as natural science, mathematics, and philosophy. Thales of Miletus (c. 625–545 BCE) is considered by some historians to be the first scientist. He sought to explain natural phenomena such as eclipses and earthquakes through general laws instead of

attributing them to the random actions of the gods, as had previously been the case.

The Greeks were interested in pure philosophy—the pursuit of understanding simply for its own sake—and it was in this spirit that they undertook their exploration of the natural world. They were not interested in applying their ideas to practical ends. The greatest philosophers were the Athenian Socrates (469–399 BCE), his student Plato (c. 428–348 BCE), and Plato's student Aristotle (384–322 BCE). They spent

In 387 BCE, Plato founded a school of philosophy and science called the Academy, which is probably the subject of this Roman mosaic dating from the 1st century CE. Plato's most celebrated pupil was the philosopher Aristotle.

their time thinking and disputing about ideal worlds, not the real world. Men of wealth and culture did not concern themselves with applied sciences such as engineering and technology: these were the preserve of craftsmen and workers, who either belonged to the lower classes or were slaves. Despite the flowering of Greek culture, there was relatively little technological progress over the centuries, and new ideas about natural science did not impact directly on everyday life.

Today we recognize the Greeks' architectural achievements, especially their awe-inspiring temples. But even in architecture, the Greeks did not invent radical new technologies, but focused on refining workmanship and perfecting forms according to mathematical principles. Civic pride was strong and the city-states, especially Athens, were wealthy, so architecture tended to be public and to serve as monumental art.

Medicine

In one area of science—medicine—the Greeks do not appear to have separated philosophy from practical matters. Medicine remains in our times a mixture of science, technology, and art. Each disease has a specific, biological cause that is the same in all cases, but each person suffering from that disease is a unique individual and reacts to the disease differently. By observing experienced physicians, student doctors learn how to approach the diagnosis and treatment of each case that presents itself. This method goes all the way

An Athenian doctor examines his patient. The Greeks were the first to develop medicine as a scientific discipline. Doctors were encouraged to make careful observations of symptoms.

⊗ PYTHAGORAS

Pythagoras of Samos (c. 580–500 BCE) introduced mathematics into natural science. He believed that mathematical principles underlay the universe and set up a school devoted to the study of numbers. He and his followers made many important discoveries—our word "calculate" (from *calculus*, Greek for pebble) derives from their practice of representing numbers as lines, triangles, or squares of pebbles placed on the ground. Much of modern mathematical thought—which underlies many scientific and technological applications—comes from Pythagoras.

He is remembered in the theorem that bears his name, which explains the relationship between the lengths of the sides of a right triangle (see diagram below). Long before Pythagoras, Babylonian and Egyptian thinkers knew there was something special about right triangles and used them when surveying land. They knew, for example, that a right triangle whose sides measured 3 and 4 units has a hypotenuse of 5 units, and that $3^2 + 4^2 = 5^2$. But it was Pythagoras and his followers who first devised a general formula to show the relationship of the triangle's sides and who discovered that this relationship is true for all right triangles, no matter what their dimensions.

A right triangle has one angle that measures 90 degrees; the side opposite the right angle is the hypotenuse. The Pythagorean thereom states that in a right triangle the square of the length of the hypotenuse equals the sum of the squares of the lengths of the other two sides. This is shown in the diagram where the number of blocks, representing the length of the side squared, alongside the hypotenuse (c) is equal to all the blocks alongside a and b. The theorem can be written as the formula: $c^2 = a^2 + b^2$

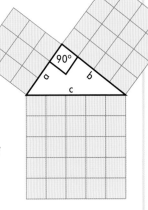

This 3rd-century BCE Italian plate depicts a war elephant. Hellenistic armies put elephants to use after Alexander's men first faced these animals in India in 326 BCE.

back to the ancient Greeks. Many experts consider that Hippocrates of Cos (c. 460–370 BCE) was the first doctor, rather than a folk healer or a medicine man. He believed that sickness could be explained rationally, and it was not something brought about by the displeasure of the gods or possession by demons. He tried to combine philosophical theories of health with careful observation and reasoning, and taught that doctors should interfere as little as possible with natural processes of healing. Doctors graduating from medical school today still use a code of medical ethics–the "Hippocratic oath"–which is based on his teachings.

THE HELLENISTIC WORLD

By the end of the Persian wars in 448 BCE, many Greek city-states had begun to resent the dominating role assumed by Athens, and it was not long before war between the Greek city-states broke out again. The long series of battles between Athens and Sparta, known as the Peloponnesian War (431–404 BCE), was eventually won by Sparta, but both sides were fatally weakened by the fighting. War and emigration had left the city-states short of citizens to fill their armies. They had to rely on mercenaries but lacked the money to pay them.

The Macedonians, a Greek-speaking people from just to the north of Greece, were quick to take advantage of this situation. Under their king

Philip II (reigned 356–336 BCE) they conquered the Greek city-states in a series of campaigns between 354 and 338 BCE. Philip was an admirer of Greek culture: he even had the philosopher Aristotle tutor his son, Alexander. Philip was also a brilliant military tactician. He adopted and improved the phalanx, and discovered how to use it effectively in large campaigns alongside the traditional Macedonian cavalry. The Macedonians could put more men into the field than the Greeks and were known as fierce fighters and great horsemen. With Greece defeated, Philip may have had plans to conquer Persia, but he died before he could do so.

Philip's son was perhaps the greatest general the world has ever seen—he is known to history as Alexander the Great (356–323 BCE). He became king at age 20, and immediately put down a rebellion in Greece and then invaded Persia. He swiftly conquered Anatolia, the Levant, and Egypt before defeating the Persian king Darius III in 331. He then led his army on a three-year campaign to conquer the whole of the Persian empire as far as Afghanistan, and even made forays into the Indian subcontinent. When he died suddenly at Babylon in 323, Alexander was only 33.

Alexander's legacy

The vast empire created by Alexander did not survive long after his death. His leading generals divided up his territories into kingdoms for themselves. These kingdoms were focused on the traditional power regions—Mesopotamia, Egypt,

The Persian king Darius III flees in terror in his chariot from Alexander's headlong charge at the battle of Gaugamela (in present-day Iraq) in 331 BCE. The victory was decisive: within a year, Alexander had swept on to capture the Persian capital, Persopolis. This is a detail from the Alexander Mosaic, made for a rich Roman in the 1st century CE and found in the House of the Faun at Pompeii, Italy.

61

ARCHIMEDES: A PRACTICAL SCIENTIST

The most famous of the late Hellenistic scientists was Archimedes (c. 287–212 BCE), who lived in the city-state of Syracuse, Sicily. An outstanding mathematician, he is often considered to be the world's first engineer because he used his scientific discoveries as the basis for practical inventions. These included the Archimedean screw (a pump), and a crane for lifting huge weights. He also came up with a scheme to set fire to enemy ships by using large mirrors to focus the sun's rays.

His most famous contribution is known as Archimedes' principle, which states that a body immersed in fluid is buoyed up by a force equal to the weight of the fluid displaced by that body. Archimedes is said to have arrived at this idea as he emerged from his bath, at which he ran jubilantly through the streets, naked, crying "Eureka" ("I have found it!").

In the early 1800s, French scientist Georges Louis Leclerc de Buffon recreated and tested Archimedes' war mirrors, which focus the sun's rays on an enemy target (such as a ship) and start a fire.

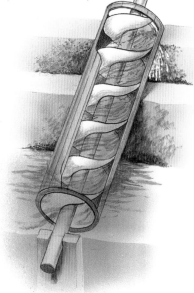

The Archimedean screw, also called the water snail, makes use of a long spiral positioned inside a cylinder. Turning the handle at one end moves water or grain from one level to another. Several gigantic Archimedean screws are used to pump water and keep the land dry at the Meadowlands Stadium in New Jersey, outside New York City.

Archimedes' death during the siege of Syracuse is depicted on a Roman mosaic. The mathematician is supposed to have ignored a challenge by a Roman soldier while engrossed in a problem of geometry. According to legend, Archimedes' last words were "Don't disturb my circles!"

and Greece. For the next century and a half these kingdoms warred with one another and with smaller kingdoms that broke away, and even with individual city-states.

All the same, Alexander's conquests had a huge and lasting impact. They meant that large parts of western Eurasia were now ruled by Macedonian elites who followed Classical Greek culture. Even where local dynasties remained, they were strongly influenced by Greek ideas. For example, in one of the most remote of these kingdoms, at Ai Khanum in Bactria (Afghanistan), archaeologists have found the remains of a Greek theater, library, and sports arena. Trade networks continued and even expanded, and the language of trade was now Greek, spreading the Greek alphabet far and wide. Greek ideas came to be applied to a greater range of cultural and economic settings. This culture that spanned western Eurasia is referred to as Hellenistic (from *Hellene*, the word the Greeks used to describe themselves).

Science was still considered to be an upper-class pursuit without practical application. This is well illustrated by the steam engine, known as the *aeolipile*, invented by the 1st-century CE mathematician Hero of Alexandria as a toy to amuse his friends. We know about these and other devices such as a water organ because Hero describes them in his writings on mechanics. They were never put to practical use.

On the other hand, the cross-currents of Greek and Asian cultures bore fruit in certain areas. Some scientists realized that that the skill of craftsmen could be applied to building intricate astronomical clocks that modeled the movements of the planets. Warfare was another area where science and technology were brought together. Craftsmen and architects competed for commissions from the rulers of Hellenistic kingdoms to build the largest and fastest ships, the highest and strongest walls, or the best catapult. The state that benefited the most from these developments was Rome, then a small city-state that soon developed into a vast empire.

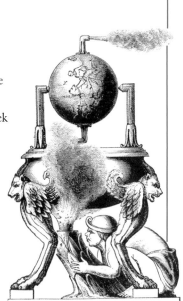

The *aeolipile* ("wind ball") invented by Hero of Alexandria was an early steam engine, but it was not put to practical use. Steam from a boiling cauldron of water (decorated with lions' heads) was channelled through two vertical pipes into a sphere. The steam escaped from the sphere through the two nozzles at top and bottom. The force of the jets of steam made the sphere rotate.

THE ROMANS

From humble beginnings as a small city-state, Rome grew into an empire that at its height reached all the way from Scotland in the north to Egypt in the south, and from Portugal in the west to Mesopotamia (Iraq) in the east. The challenges of conquering and governing this vast territory stimulated Roman ingenuity, resulting in new technologies and Romanized versions of old ones. By the fall of Rome in the 5th century CE, the Romans had created some of the most impressive engineering feats of the ancient world.

According to Roman tradition, the twin brothers Romulus and Remus–who had been abandoned at birth and raised by a wolf–founded Rome in 753 BCE. Archaeological evidence suggests Rome began as a farming settlement on a hill beside the Tiber River during the 10th century BCE. By about 800 BCE, it had grown into a town.

The people who occupied this settlement were the Latins, one of many different peoples living in Italy at this time. The Latins lived in Latium, a part of central Italy. The Etruscans were the most important of the non-Latins. They lived to the north of Latium, in Etruria, the part of Italy roughly equivalent to modern Tuscany. Active seafarers and traders, the Etruscans were in close contact with the Greeks and had developed the first urban civilization in western Europe (see box on page 66). Other

The inscription on this coin of the 2nd century BCE reads *provoco* ("I appeal"). A basic privilege of citizenship during the republic was the *provocatio*, the right of people to appeal or challenge a law by speaking out.

non-Latin peoples included the Greeks, who occupied trading colonies on the southern Italian peninsula.

Although primarily farmers, the Latins of Rome also traded salt with their Etruscan and Greek neighbors, from whom they acquired knowledge of iron and chariots. Greek culture and technology strongly influenced the Etruscans and early Romans. Both adopted the alphabet from the Greeks, together with ideas about military tactics, religion, and politics.

Our knowledge of the history of early Rome comes from the writings of later Roman historians like Livy (59 BCE–17 CE). These accounts were written some 500 years after the events they describe. This would be the same as if the only accounts historians had of Columbus's arrival in the New World had been written in the late 20th century.

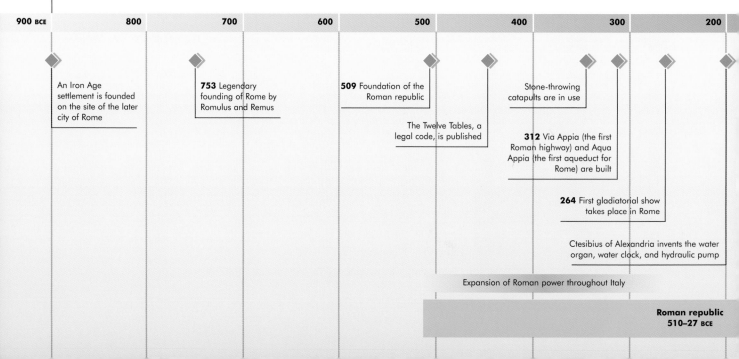

900 BCE	800	700	600	500	400	300	200

An Iron Age settlement is founded on the site of the later city of Rome

753 Legendary founding of Rome by Romulus and Remus

509 Foundation of the Roman republic

The Twelve Tables, a legal code, is published

Stone-throwing catapults are in use

312 Via Appia (the first Roman highway) and Aqua Appia (the first aqueduct for Rome) are built

264 First gladiatorial show takes place in Rome

Ctesibius of Alexandria invents the water organ, water clock, and hydraulic pump

Expansion of Roman power throughout Italy

Roman republic 510–27 BCE

THE ROMAN REPUBLIC

According to these later histories, Rome was initially ruled by a king, who had religious, political, judicial, and military functions. In 510 BCE a group of patricians (aristocrats descended from the "founding fathers" whom Romulus is supposed to have chosen as his advisers) overthrew the monarch, and created a republic (*res publica*, "public things"). Power now passed into the hands of the patricians. To prevent any person or family assuming total control of the government, each year the patricians elected two consuls, who were given responsibility for the day-to-day running of the republic. Each consul had the power to veto the decisions of the other, ensuring that neither man could become a dictator.

The plebs, or plebeians, made up the mass of Rome's citizens. A plebeian was anyone who lacked noble birth and was thus excluded from the senate, the council of patricians that met to debate and make policy. In 494 BCE the plebs formed their own assembly, the *concilium plebis*, and elected their own officers, the tribunes. The plebs now had an effective voice in government to balance against the patricians. In about 450 BCE the publication of a legal code, the Twelve Tables, strengthened the position of the plebs still further by confirming the equal rights of all free citizens.

This bronze statue, known as the Capitoline wolf, symbolizes Rome's mythical origins. According to legend, the she-wolf raised the twins Romulus and Remus, who were sons of the god Mars. The twins founded Rome on hills overlooking the Tiber River in 753 BCE.

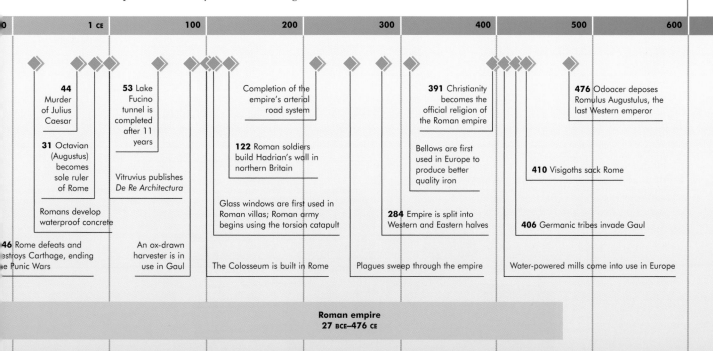

0	1 CE	100	200	300	400	500	600

44 Murder of Julius Caesar

53 Lake Fucino tunnel is completed after 11 years

Completion of the empire's arterial road system

391 Christianity becomes the official religion of the Roman empire

476 Odoacer deposes Romulus Augustulus, the last Western emperor

31 Octavian (Augustus) becomes sole ruler of Rome

Vitruvius publishes *De Re Architectura*

122 Roman soldiers build Hadrian's wall in northern Britain

Bellows are first used in Europe to produce better quality iron

410 Visigoths sack Rome

Romans develop waterproof concrete

Glass windows are first used in Roman villas; Roman army begins using the torsion catapult

284 Empire is split into Western and Eastern halves

406 Germanic tribes invade Gaul

46 Rome defeats and destroys Carthage, ending the Punic Wars

An ox-drawn harvester is in use in Gaul

The Colosseum is built in Rome

Plagues sweep through the empire

Water-powered mills come into use in Europe

Roman empire
27 BCE–476 CE

Map labels (geographic features and cities):

Silchester △ London
Cologne ■
Reims ■ Trier ■ Mainz ■
Metz ▲
Seine
Rhine
Danube
Augsburg ■
Carnuntum ▲■
CARPA...
Autun ▲ Augst △ Windisch △
Budapest ■△
Tisza
Loire
Lyon ■ ▲
Aîme ▲
Susa ▲
Milan △
Virunum ■
Sava
Sarmizegethusa ■
Bordeaux ■
Saintes ▲
Po
Pula △
Danu...
Kostolac ■
DINARIC ALPS
BALKA...
Nîmes ▲ St-Rémy △
Béziers ▲ Cimiez ■
Narbonne ■
Rhône
Salonae △
PYRENEES
Tarragona ▲
Corsica
Aleria ■
Rome ▲▲
Thessalonica ■▲
Douro
Ebro
Coimbra ■
Segovia ▲
Pollensa ▲
Palma ■
Benevento ■
Pompeii △
Tagus
Toledo ▲
Mérida ■△
Córdoba ■
Italica △
Balearic Islands
Sardinia
Cagliari ▲
Nicopolis ▲
Corinth ▲
Tangiers ■
Cherchell ▲▲
Djemila ▲ Constantine ▲
Carthage ▲■
Dougga ▲
El Jem ▲▲
Timgad ▲
Sicily
Syracuse ■
Mediterranean Sea
Crete
Moulouya
Leptis Magna ▲■
Cyrene ■△

The map shows the stages by which the Roman empire reached its greatest extent in 117 CE, at the death of the emperor Trajan. A succession of military victories had turned a small city-state into the major power in the Mediterranean, Middle East, Near East, and much of northern Europe. Also shown are major cities, and the locations of three defining Roman structures: amphitheaters, raised aqueducts, and triumphal arches.

⊗ THE ETRUSCANS

The Etruscans are one of the mysterious peoples of the ancient world. Their language was unrelated to any of the languages spoken in most of Europe, and though they have left some written inscriptions, these are generally short and difficult to decipher.

Compared to the other peoples living in Italy prior to the Romans, the Etruscans were technologically sophisticated. They planned their towns in a checkerboard fashion and enclosed them with sturdy stone walls. Farm fields were irrigated and well drained. And they mined iron, copper, and tin by digging deep shafts and tunnels, and traded objects made from these metals throughout Italy and beyond.

Much of our knowledge of Etruscan life comes from aristocratic tombs, which were built in the form of houses. This tomb sculpture shows a deceased husband and wife reclining on couches as if ready for a banquet.

The constitution as it was developed in the first century of the republic provided a system of checks and balances between classes. It established a community of interests that gave Rome its political energy and stability. Rome now began to expand from a small city-state into something altogether larger.

The expansion of Rome

In 510 BCE the city of Rome controlled a surrounding territory of about 317 square miles (822 sq. km). It extended its dominance over all of Italy through a combination of effective military control and steady consolidation. The key to Rome's expansion was its army, which originated as a part-time citizen-militia made up of landowning farmers. With their political and land rights protected both by written law and elected representatives, these men were willing to

The growth of the Roman empire

○ area under Etruscan influence, c.600 BCE

expansion of Roman control

▨ limit of Rome, c.500 BCE
▨ gains by 100 BCE
▨ gains by 117 CE

△ site of amphitheater
▲ site of aqueduct
▲ site of triumphal arch
■ provincial capital

0   600 km
0   400 mi

Black Sea

Byzantium
Izmit
Ankara
Yesil
Kayseri
Kizil Irmak
Lake Tuz
na
phesos
Aspendus
Selimiye
Tarsus
Antakya
Orontes
Euphrates
Myra
Cyprus
Hamah
Palmyra
Paphos
Syrian Desert
Caesarea
Busra ash Sham
Jerusalem
Alexandria

leave their farms to serve in the army for short periods as required. However, as the Romans acquired more territory, the state needed a larger, permanent army, and men were enlisted from the lower classes as career soldiers. In addition, the Romans recruited new troops by promising conquered people Roman citizenship in return for military service.

The army was organized in units called legions. A legion included 3,000 to 5,000 troops, most of whom were heavily armed foot soldiers, backed up by cavalry units and various types of catapult, which fired stones or iron bolts (see pages 68–69). Initially, the Romans adopted the phalanx formation of armored spearmen used by the Greeks (see this volume, pages 19–21), but later replaced it with a more flexible formation

better suited to fighting with new weapons—the *pilum* (a throwing spear consisting of an iron head fitted to a wooden shaft), and the *gladius* (a short, thrusting sword of iron). All infantry soldiers carried a sword and wooden shield, and they wore iron chest armor, iron shin guards (greaves), and a bronze or iron crested helmet.

Roman soldiers were trained never to give up, and they gave Rome a reputation for being able to bounce back from military defeats through a persistent will to win. By 264 BCE Rome had subdued most of Italy and was looking for new conquests overseas. It decided to challenge the power of Carthage, in north Africa. Carthage was founded by the Phoenicians but was an independent city-state by 264 BCE. It headed a great maritime empire, with colonies in Sicily, Sardinia, and Spain.

To mount their challenge to Carthage, the Romans needed to acquire a navy. In only a few months they built and manned a fleet of 100 large warships of a Carthaginian design called a quinquereme, in which five rowers worked each oar. After three savage wars with Carthage (the Punic Wars), the Romans finally triumphed in 146 BCE. The Punic Wars brought the Romans control of the western Mediterranean.

Further gains followed. By the 1st century BCE, Rome had conquered all the Greek city-states in southern Italy and Sicily, and had gained control of the Balkans, Greece, and much of Anatolia (Asia Minor).

Troubled times

The acquisition of these far-flung provinces upset the delicate balance of the Roman republic. Aristocrats grew wealthy not only on the loot captured in wars abroad but also by buying up land in the new provinces. They then invested their wealth in agricultural property in Italy, forcing peasant farmers off their land. The large numbers of dispossessed farmers who migrated to Rome swelled the city's growing numbers. Rome relied on food imports—especially wheat—to feed its population, which by the 1st century BCE had risen to one-half million. Frequent food

The centurion, a non-commissioned officer, was vital to the efficient running of the Roman army. In charge of a *century* of 80 soldiers, he was responsible for maintaining his unit's discipline and supervising his men in battle. He is shown here with his sword (*gladius*) and vinewood staff, both of which he used to discipline the troops of his century.

Continues on page 70

MILITARY TECHNOLOGY

T he Romans paid great attention to developing better artillery
weapons (such as the crossbow and *ballista*, or catapult) as
well as "engines of war" (such as siege towers). Many books
have survived on military subjects, revealing that there was clearly
great interest in military technology. For example, in his account of
conquering Gaul (*The Gallic Wars*), the general Julius Caesar
(100–42 BCE) included an extensive description of the pontoon
bridge he had his men build over the Rhine.

One of the most accurate records we have of Roman military
technology comes from Trajan's Column in Rome. This monument,
some 125 feet (38 m) high, was erected by the emperor Trajan
(reigned 97–117 CE) to celebrate his military successes against the
Dacians, inhabitants of what is now Romania. The spiral band of
carved reliefs that decorates the column shows the Roman army at
work—fighting, marching, building bridges and camps.

The Roman army employed several forms of battle artillery. The
first was the *manuballista* (hand-held crossbow). This weapon
originated in China some time in the 4th century BCE (see this
volume, page 22), and came to the Romans via the Persians and
Greeks. It consisted of a bow mounted on a wooden support (the
stock) with a trigger mechanism, and the archer used not only the
muscles in his arms but also his legs and back to pull back the
bowstring. Because the tension exerted on a crossbow's bowstring is
much greater than that of a conventional bow, a crossbow could
shoot arrows accurately over longer distances than an ordinary bow.

The *carroballista* (torsion or mounted crossbow) derived its power
from two skeins of human hair or animal sinew held in drums
mounted on either side of a wooden stock. These skeins were twisted
to produce torsion and store energy (the same thing happens when
you twist a rubber band). Each skein had a horizontal wooden arm
inserted in it and a bowstring that joined the two arms. Soldiers
placed a projectile—a stone, arrow, or iron bolt—at the center of the
bowstring, which they winched back by turning the arms. When they
released the bowstring, the skeins suddenly and violently unwound,
propelling the projectile forward. According to the military commen-
tator Vegetius, writing in the late 4th century CE, a legion typically
had 55 *carroballista*, with 11 men assigned to each weapon.

Late in Roman history, a new *ballista* appeared, known as an
onager ("wild ass") for its kicking action. A thick skein of cords
was stretched horizontally between a strong frame and a vertical

throwing arm. At the end of this arm was a sling containing a heavy
stone. Soldiers used a winch to pull down the arm, which was held
by a catch until released with the tap of a mallet. The *onager* was
able to hurl stones about 500 yards (450 m).

The Roman army included engineers to construct forts, watch-
towers, and roads. Permanent frontiers were built in some parts
of the empire to keep the Barbarians out and control the local
population. In northern Britain, Hadrian's Wall ran for 70 miles
(110 km) from coast to coast. Built of stone for its entire length, the
wall was 8–10 feet (2.5–3 m) wide and up to 21 feet (6.5 m) high. It
was an impressive monument to Roman engineering skills.

Roman officers deployed their well-trained, well-disciplined troops in a variety of formations. The testudo (tortoise) was adopted when an army was approaching the heavily defended walls of a fortress or facing a hail of enemy arrows or other missiles. The legionaries at the front, back, and sides held their shields edge to edge facing outward while those in the center raised their shields above their heads to deflect the enemy's missiles, as shown in this marble relief from Trajan's Column, a monument erected in Rome to celebrate a successful military campaign by the emperor Trajan.

One of the Romans' long-range artillery weapons was the carroballista (above), which worked like an enormous crossbow. It gave assault troops covering fire during siege warfare.

The Romans had a variety of artillery pieces for short- and long-range fighting. The diagram below shows five of them, together with their estimated ranges.

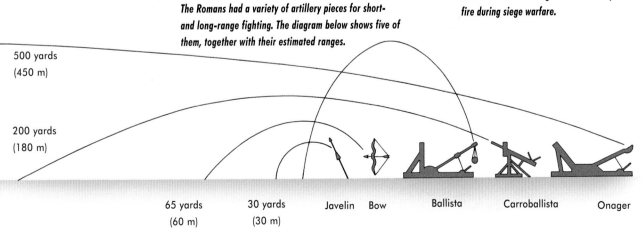

500 yards
(450 m)

200 yards
(180 m)

65 yards
(60 m)

30 yards
(30 m)

Javelin Bow Ballista Carroballista Onager

shortages increased class conflict. This situation led to a series of civil wars in which one leader after another played to the sympathies of either the aristocrats or the plebs.

Triumphs abroad were the route to political success at home. Wars brought a constant stream of booty and plunder. Some generals, such as Sulla (137–78 BCE), Pompey (106–48 BCE), and Julius Caesar (100–42 BCE) gained political power by forming armies loyal to them to conquer new territory. They funded grandiose public building projects in Rome but did little to improve the living conditions of the poor.

After conquering Gaul (France) in 49 BCE, Julius Caesar defiantly led his army into Rome, bringing an end to the republic. The senate gave him the office of dictator for life, with virtually unlimited powers. Some factions feared Caesar wanted to bring a return to kingship, and a group of conspirators assassinated him in 44 BCE.

The end of the republic

Another, even more devastating, civil war followed the death of Julius Caesar. It ended after 13 years of bloodshed when Caesar's grand-nephew Octavian (63 BCE–14 CE), whom Caesar had named as his heir, made himself master of Rome. In 27 BCE the senate gave Octavian the name by which he is now generally known, Augustus ("revered one"). His successors called themselves *imperator* ("commander-in-chief"), which gives us the English word "emperor."

Augustus made far-reaching changes to the way the empire was governed. In part, he preserved republican traditions by sharing power with the senate. Although he appointed governors for the newly acquired provinces, he left it to the senate to manage the affairs of the older ones. By sharing power once again with the aristocratic families, Augustus reduced the dangers of civil war.

After a humiliating defeat in Germany in 9 CE, Augustus abandoned further territorial conquest. But the empire continued to grow under his successors until it reached its fullest extent in the reign of Trajan (98–117 CE).

The reign of Augustus brought much needed peace and stability to Rome, a fact that Augustus himself chose to celebrate by commissioning the Altar of Augustan Peace in 13 BCE. This panel from the altar shows senators taking part in a procession.

TECHNOLOGY IN ROMAN SOCIETY

During the first two centuries CE, the economy of the Roman empire flourished as a result of the political and social stability created by Augustus and his successors. Within this stable environment, the Romans chose to pursue the development of certain kinds of technology. Historians have sometimes criticized the Romans for not inventing more technological devices, but their real genius lay in shaping existing technology to support the ideal Roman citizen— a landed gentleman who was civic-minded, politically active, and sympathetic to the military.

A nation of gentlemen farmers

In the Roman world, land was the measure of social and economic success. Because the Romans imagined themselves to be a society that began as a nation of farmers and saw the land as the sustaining source of Roman virtues, the ideal citizen was a gentleman with a large agricultural estate. His substantial income, derived from his tenant farmers' rents, gave him the necessary leisure to think and to participate in civic affairs. As the Roman writer Cicero (106–43 BCE) advised his son in *On Duties*:

"Nothing is better than agriculture, nothing more profitable, nothing more pleasurable, nothing more worthy of a free man." People who made their fortunes through trade or military booty often used their wealth to buy land and withdraw from commercial life.

This emphasis on living off the wealth of one's estate prompted Romans to take an interest in agriculture. Roman landowners investigated new crops and new techniques for processing wine grapes, olives, and other foodstuffs. At the same time, though, the Romans were slow to invest in labor-saving agricultural implements—if a landed aristrocrat had surplus wealth, he preferred to use it to buy more land and not to develop new machines.

Commonwealth and spectacle

The Roman state represented all classes of Roman society—an ideal embodied in the four initials of the official motto of Rome: SPQR (*senatus populusque Romanis*: "the senate and people of Rome"). In other words, the Roman republic was a commonwealth—its purpose was to safeguard the common well-being of the Roman people. To realize this vision of a commonwealth, to confirm their social status, and to make sure that they retained the support of the people who voted them into political office, Roman aristocrats frequently spent their surplus wealth on civic projects such as monuments, public buildings, or aqueducts—channels for carrying water to cities from rivers and lakes some distance away (see pages 80–81 and 84). For instance, to celebrate Rome's victories over Carthage and the Greek city of Corinth in 144 BCE, the senate used war booty to construct a 55-mile (88-km) aqueduct, the Aqua Marcia, which provided water for the growing city of Rome. In contrast to many other societies, ancient and modern, technology was something to be used in the service of the state to the benefit of all, not just to enrich the ruling elite.

As role models for other Roman aristocrats, the emperors exemplified this tradition of sponsoring public works. Augustus justifiably claimed to have transformed Rome from a city of brick to one of marble. He carried out a vast program of public building, including the construction of a new

The Forum, a complex of temples, courthouses, assembly halls, and marketplaces, was the center of Rome's political, business, and religious life throughout most of its history. Even in ruins, it reflects the splendor and strength of the city and its empire.

Forum, a complex of buildings that was the center of Roman life. His successors in the 1st and 2nd centuries CE were able to draw on the vast resources of the Roman state to order the construction of new cities, harbors, roads, aqueducts, public monuments, baths, and amphitheaters. For example, the emperor Claudius (reigned 41–54 CE) authorized the construction of a tunnel to control the water level of Lake Fucino in Italy.

Located high up in the Apennine Mountains, Lake Fucino was not drained by a river, and so heavy rains sometimes caused it to flood the farms along its shoreline. Some 30,000 workers spent 11 years digging a 3½-mile (5.5-km) tunnel from the lake to a nearby river—the longest underground tunnel in the world until 1876. For most of the tunnel's route, workers used picks and shovels to excavate a shallow trench, which they bricked over and buried with soil. At one point, however, the workers had to cut through more than a mile (1.6 km) of solid rock, using only hammers and chisels.

The provision of spectacles was also considered part of the role of ideal citizen, so along with civil engineering projects, the emperor and leading citizens paid for elaborate religious festivals and popular events like gladiatorial contests, animal fights, and military parades. These were intended to attract huge audiences, and Roman engineers—trained largely in the army—busied themselves designing amphitheaters and stadiums. It is here that Roman technological ingenuity came into full play. For instance, when Claudius arranged for an elaborate mock naval battle to be staged in Rome to entertain the people, a huge artificial lake called a *naumachia* was built for the occasion using specially hardened watertight concrete (see page 81).

Most impressive of all was Rome's amphitheater, the Colosseum, completed in 80 CE. Standing 165 feet (50 m) high, it contained tiers of seats for more than 50,000 spectators and was designed to allow them to move quickly and

THE WATER ORGAN

The water organ, or *hydraulis*, illustrates the Romans' fascination with ingenious mechanical devices. The ancestor of the modern pipe organ, this musical instrument was based on the traditional panpipes (a row of reed pipes that the player blows across to produce musical notes). It used compressed air to make the sounds mechanically. Ctesibius, who lived in Alexandria, Egypt, in the 3rd century BCE, may have invented it. Books by the 1st-century CE Greek mathematician Hero of Alexandria and the Roman engineer and architect Marcus Pollio Vitruvius (1st century CE)

A detail from a 2nd-century CE mosaic shows musicians playing the water organ and cornu, or Roman horn.

describe the organ's mechanics. The organist raised a lever to push down a piston that pumped air into an inverted metal bowl immersed in water. The increased air pressure in the bowl forced the water out, raising the level of water in the surrounding tank, and this in turn pushed air out of the top of the tank and into a hollow chest supporting a row of pipes. Wooden slide valves controlled the flow of air from the pipe chest into the individual pipes. As in a modern pipe organ, the musician depressed a key on a keyboard to move the slide and open the flow of air.

The water organ appealed greatly to the Romans' love of the spectacular, and they adopted it with great enthusiasm, perfecting its design and putting it to all kinds of uses. Mechanical music was played regularly in theaters and amphitheaters to accompany gladiatorial battles, games, processions, weddings, and even the swearing-in of public officials.

consequently there was ongoing interest in military matters. From the early days of the republic, military duty was seen as part of the citizen's role, but by the time of the emperors the army was staffed by professional soldiers. For them, a lifelong military career was the path to upward mobility and a better life.

Free and slave labor

The course of technological change in the Roman empire was also shaped by the presence of a large workforce. As the empire expanded, wealth from newly conquered territories allowed the rich to get richer, eliminated the class of free farmers, and created large numbers of poor people in the city and countryside. During most of the empire's history, therefore, there was always an ample supply of workers ready to work for low wages on agricultural estates and building projects.

The Romans added to this labor supply by enslaving conquered peoples and bringing these slaves back to work in Italy. Many slaves were employed in the least desirable and most dangerous jobs, such as mining for metals or rowing galley ships. However, slaves captured in the Greek provinces were often well educated and served as tutors, doctors, and craftsmen. The Roman aristocracy enjoyed the products of crafts-manship—sculpture, mosaics, pottery, silverware, and glass vessels—but they looked down on the people who made these objects. So slaves were trained in these crafts.

Historians estimate that at the close of the 1st century BCE there were 2 to 3 million slaves in Italy—accounting for about 40 percent of the population. Except for house servants in the cities, slavery was never as wide-spread in the provinces as it was in Italy.

Emperors called on the expertise of their engineers to provide ever-more impressive entertainments for the masses. This drawing of the 15th-century Italian Renaissance shows one of the naval battles staged in the Colosseum as part of the festivities held to mark the building's opening in 80 CE.

easily in and out through approximately 80 entrances and the same number of stairways. It took only about five minutes to empty the building. Brackets and sockets on top of the walls supported masts from which a gigantic awning, the *velarium*, was suspended for shade. The vast arena was used for gladiatorial combats and animal spectacles; a system of trapdoors below the wooden floor permitted crowd-pleasing special effects such as the simultaneous appearance of up to 64 wild animals. The arena could also be flooded for mock naval battles.

Warfare was another area of technology that received a great deal of attention (see pages 68–69). Rome had acquired its territory and power through its military might, and

The Roman empire relied on slaves to carry out heavy work. This tombstone relief from the 3rd century CE depicts slaves at work quarrying and transporting marble.

A 3rd-century CE mosaic depicts farm workers sowing and plowing. Farmers used the *aratrum*, a light plow pulled by oxen, to turn over the light soils of the Mediterranean region. The plowman is goading the oxen with a stick to make them work harder.

classes were free to concentrate on their social roles, and they gave little thought to using technology to increase agricultural productivity. Instead, the Romans exploited the fertile regions of the territories they conquered (for example in Egypt, north Africa, Spain, and Gaul) to increase their supply of cereals and other produce.

Agricultural yields rose steadily between roughly 100 BCE and 100 CE, providing the necessary surplus to feed the growing population of Rome and the empire's other cities. When the prosperity of the empire began to decline in the 3rd century CE, the Romans turned to technology such as waterwheels to boost food production, but by then it was too late (see page 89).

The staple diet of most Romans was bread and *pulmentum*, a gruel of coarsely ground wheat flour similar to the cornmeal polenta of today. Romans also ate olives, olive oil, honey, fruit, and occasionally cheese. Fish and shellfish such as oysters provided protein; meat was a luxury only eaten on special occasions. Wine was an essential part of a meal. Roman soldiers demanded a daily ration of wine along with their bread.

Roman aristocrats had a much wider choice of food and came to appreciate fine cooking. As the empire grew rich and absorbed ideas from Greece and the East, these wealthy Romans took to eating sumptuous meals in a reclining position on couches. Critics of this lifestyle made great play of the exotic dishes served at banquets, such as elephant tails or roasted dormice.

As long as cheap labor, both free and slave, was widely available, the Romans had little need to create machines that reduced the amount of work needed to perform a particular task. Nor did it make sense for wealthy Romans to spend money on perfecting new machines that might put people out of work; doing so, they reasoned, might lead the poor to revolt and upset the social order. Hence, if one wanted to increase one's wealth, it was better to invest in more land and employ more workers or slaves. And besides, society deemed it desirable for the rich to spend their surplus fortune on civic projects or public spectacles.

AGRICULTURE

Latin writers regularly celebrated farming and the life of the countryside as the source of all virtue. Because the Romans perceived themselves as sprung from a nation of farmers, they took a great interest in managing their agricultural estates. As long as there was a large labor supply to grow and process food, the Roman upper

Wheat cultivation

The Romans used the dry-farming techniques (farming without irrigation) that were common to all the lands of the Mediterranean region. They understood the importance of using fertilizers to maintain soil fertility and added both animal manure and lime (calcium oxide made by roasting chalk or limestone) to their fields. Italy and most of the Mediterranean area has thin, dry soils, so the Romans prepared the ground with a lightweight plow called an *aratrum*, along with hoes and spades. They harvested crops with

A relief carving shows farm workers operating a *vallus*, a reaping machine developed by the Romans. So far as is known, the machine was only used on the broad, flat plains of northeastern Gaul.

WINE AND OLIVE OIL

The Romans systematically developed different types of grapes for wine production by using sophisticated techniques for cutting and grafting one type of grape plant onto another. In Gaul, they adapted grape varieties to the climates of different regions. Several famous wine-producing regions in France—for instance, Burgundy, Bordeaux, and Alsace—owe their origins to the Romans. The Romans often flavored their wine by adding resins (as is still done in Greece today to make retsina), or by storing it in lead containers—a practice that contaminated the wine and poisoned those who drank it habitually.

Olive trees were grown, then as now, in all the countries of the Mediterranean region. On small farms peasants crushed both wine grapes and olives in the traditional way, by treading on them barefoot. Over time the beam press came into use on large estates. This consisted of a large horizontal beam that was hinged to the wall at one end. A counterweight was fastened to the other end. Bags of the grapes or olives to be crushed were placed under the beam, and a windlass (a rope wound around a barrel or drum) was used to lower and raise the counterweight.

At some point the Romans invented the screw press for use on smaller farms. The grapes or olives were placed underneath a horizontal plate that could be moved up and down by turning a large screw. As the screw was tightened, it exerted great pressure on the grapes or olives, crushing them.

A mosaic from Gaul shows two workers operating an olive oil press. While one man pulls back on a pivoted pole, the other attaches a counterweight, so that the bag of pressed olives can be hauled up.

curved sickles, similar to those used on American and European farms until the 19th century.

A farming invention, developed by the Romans in Gaul, was the *vallus*, an ox-drawn harvester that could do the work of several men. The natural historian, Pliny the Elder (23–79 CE), gives this description of the machine: "On the vast estates of the Gauls, an enormous box with teeth, supported on two wheels, is moved across the crop by an ox that pushes the device; the heads of grain, torn off by the teeth, fall into the box." The *vallus* was probably developed because the short harvesting season in northern Europe made it important to be able to harvest the crops quickly. The farmers of this region were wealthy native Gauls who had become Roman citizens. They farmed large estates and lived in villas like those of Italy, with rooms built around a courtyard, heated floors, and mosaic pavements.

MINING AND METALLURGY

Land was generally treated as private property within the Roman empire. However, the rights to any minerals (such as iron and gold) beneath the surface belonged to the state, and in theory mineral deposits were to be exploited for the public good. In practice, profits from mines went to emperors or their favorites.

The Romans used slaves to carry out the highly dangerous work of mining. Because slaves were considered expendable, mines were exploited as intensively as possible with no regard to safety. Most Roman mines consisted of deep shafts in which the ore was cut underground from the mineral seam and brought to the surface on the backs of men, women, and children. When there was sufficient ventilation, miners would build fires to heat the rock, then throw cold water on it to cause cracking, which made it easier to extract the ore.

Preventing flooding

Roman engineers had to cope with the problem of flooding as they dug their deep shafts. When conditions were right, they dug adits, special drainage tunnels that carried the floodwater away. For example, at a mine in La Zarza, Spain, Roman engineers cut an adit 1 mile (1.6 km) long through solid rock to reduce flooding. In other cases, the Romans pumped water out of the mines using an Archimedean screw (see this volume, page 62). A third method was to use tread-wheels. At the copper mines in Rio Tinto,

A relief from a tombstone depicts a blacksmith hammering at the anvil (center) while his assistant uses a pair of bellows to increase the heat in the forge (left). The smith's tools, including hammer and tongs, are shown at right.

Spain, the Romans used a pair of vertical wheels on a single shaft; a man walked along the top of one wheel, and buckets on the rim of the second wheel lifted the water from one level to the next. By combining four sets of wheels, they were able to carry water nearly 100 feet (30 m) upward.

Metalworking

At the surface, metalworkers removed the metal from the ore. The Romans knew how to separate gold and silver from copper ores by melting the ores with lead. During this process, any gold and silver in the ores was taken up by the lead, leaving the copper separate. The metalworkers then melted the amalgamation of gold, silver, and lead to separate the three metals. As well as bronze—an alloy, or mixture, of copper and tin (see this volume, pages 16–18)—the Romans made brass by combining copper and zinc.

Roman smiths made wrought iron by smelting iron ore in a furnace at low temperatures and beating it on an anvil with hammers. Toward the end of the empire, the Romans developed powerful bellows for raising the temperature of the furnace. They may have occasionally melted iron by accident, but they seem never to have developed techniques for making cast iron. Cast iron is harder than wrought iron, and is produced by pouring liquid iron into molds and allowing it to harden (see this volume, pages 23–24 and 48–49).

TRANSPORTATION

One of the outstanding technological achievements of the Romans—and also the most long-lasting—was their network of paved roads. They were not the first people in the ancient world to

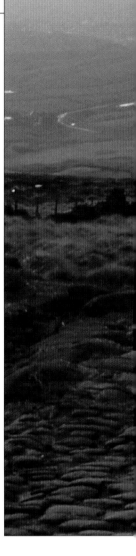

Many Roman roads, such as this one in northern England, had ruts cut into them to help wheeled traffic negotiate difficult stretches. The road network, virtually complete by 200 CE, was used mainly for military and administrative purposes, rather than transporting goods for trade.

use them—the Persian empire had a number of elaborate "royal roads," and the Etruscans had built roads between their cities in Italy. However, the Roman system was by far the largest and most sophisticated—it is estimated that the empire had as much as 56,000 miles (90,000 km) of main roads and some 125,000 miles (201,000 km) of secondary roads.

The Twelve Tables (the Roman legal code of 450 BCE) distinguished between four different types of road on the basis of their width. The *semita* (footpath) was only 1 foot (0.3 m) wide, the *iter* (for horsemen and pedestrians) 3 feet (1 m) wide, the *actus* (for a single carriage) 4 feet (1.2 m) wide, and the *via* (major highway) 8 feet (2.4 m) wide.

In republican times, highways connected Rome with its Latin colonies and played a major role in consolidating Roman control in Italy.

Ditch (fossa) · Curb stones · Large surface stones · Gravel · Bank (vallum) · Foundation of stone slabs

Roman engineers built their roads in layers, as this cross section shows. The aim was to create a well-drained, durable road surface that could be used by armies throughout the year.

⊗ MILITARY ROADS

The main function of the highways was to provide the Roman army with a network of fast routes to reach distant trouble-spots. Fully equipped legionaries on a forced march could cover up to 24 miles (39 km) in five hours along these highways. Because the army built and maintained most roads, construction skills formed an important part of military training.

The Romans used various techniques for the different classes of roads they built, but they set high technical standards for the highways. The roads were well drained and surfaced with paving slabs or cobbles so that they remained passable in every kind of weather. They were designed to take the most direct line over flat terrain and often followed the ridges of hills. Large stone slabs formed a firm foundation for the roadbed. Above this were layers of gravel and rock, with a final top layer of stone blocks placed between higher curb stones. The road surface was high in the center and lower along the outer edges so that rainwater ran off into the drainage ditches (*fossae*) at either side.

Throughout the empire, milestones set up every mile showed the distance from Rome (1 Roman mile equaled 1,000 paces, or 5,000 feet/1,525 m). All measurements were taken from a golden milestone in the city's center.

Despite good roads, travel by wheeled carts was often slow, expensive, and uncomfortable. This horse-drawn wagon was one method of transportation for passengers, but a lack of spring suspension made it an unpopular option for long-distance journeys.

Later the profits of conquest were used to extend the road network the length and breadth of the empire.

Communications

The Romans developed an efficient courier system that allowed generals and administrators in distant parts of the empire to keep in touch with Rome. Post-houses, where couriers could change horses, were sited every 10–15 miles (16–24 km) and official hostels every 20–30 miles (32–48 km).

Horses were also used to pull the light stagecoaches that carried important officials around the empire. However, horses could not be used to pull heavy loads on carts and wagons because the harnesses then in use pressed on the animal's windpipe and choked it. Oxen, which pulled heavy wagons instead, were extremely slow, and this made it extremely expensive to carry goods by road.

Harbors

One scholar has estimated that the cost of transporting goods by road was five times greater than by river boat, and 28 times greater than shipping them by sea. In other words, it was far cheaper to transport grain to Rome in huge sea-going ships than to cart it into the city from the surrounding countryside. To facilitate this trade, the Romans built artificial harbors where good natural harbors were lacking: for example, at Terracina, Civitavecchia, Pozzuoli, and Messina in Italy; Cherchel and Leptis Magna in Africa; and Frejus in southern France.

One of the largest imperial engineering projects ever undertaken was the construction of the harbor at Ostia, the port serving Rome at the mouth of the Tiber River. In 42 CE, during the reign of the emperor Claudius, engineers dredged a large harbor and built an extensive breakwater with a 200-foot (60-m)

lighthouse modeled after the Pharos lighthouse at Alexandria, Egypt. The beacon at Ostia used burning pitch and could be seen for miles at sea. In 112 CE, the emperor Trajan expanded the port by adding a hexagonal inner harbor as well as a canal connecting the port to the Tiber.

Ships and navigation

Like the Greeks, the Romans used galleys on the Mediterranean. These warships relied on one or more banks of rowers (usually slaves) to maneuver in and out of harbors, but they used square sails and wind power for the ocean-going part of the trip. The Romans improved on Greek designs by adding a second mast projecting over the bow and by using rings to attach their mainsail to the yardarm, a horizontal wooden spar attached to the mast. On the open sea, these ships could reach speeds of 4–6 knots (4½ mph or 7 km/h) with a favorable wind, but only 2–2½ knots (2½–3 mph or 4–5 km/h) with an unfavorable one.

Roman *corbitae* (merchant ships) were generally heavy. While the typical Greek ship had a capacity of 130 tons, Roman merchant vessels were able to carry 340 tons or more. One supership, described by Pliny the Elder, could even manage 1,300 tons. It was designed to carry wheat in bulk from Egypt to Ostia. But on one voyage its cargo was a 500-ton stone obelisk (a tall, needle-like Egyptian monument) that was intended to adorn the city of Rome, along with some 800 tons of lentils as ballast.

Most produce and goods went by ship. The Mediterranean was the main highway for trade, and its harbors, such as this one (right), which may be Stabiae or Pozzuoli in Italy, were prosperous and busy. River trade was also important. A tombstone of a wine trader (below) shows oarsmen rowing a barge laden with barrels of wine on the Mosel River in Gaul.

Historians know little about how Roman mariners determined their position while at sea, or even whether Romans used maps in navigation. We do know, however, that they ventured out of the Mediterranean into the Atlantic Ocean and, via the Red Sea, into the Indian Ocean and perhaps even the China Sea.

The engineer and architect Vitruvius, writing in the 1st century CE, described a paddlewheel device used on Roman ships to measure distance traveled. Paddlewheels on either side of the ship were connected by an axle running through the hull. The paddlewheels turned a system of geared drums, which caused a pebble to drop into a container to indicate each mile traveled.

BUILDING AND ENGINEERING

The Greeks exerted a profound influence on Roman architecture. The Romans adopted the Greek temple style as their own, and then improved on it. Greek buildings were constructed by placing a horizontal beam (lintel) between two vertical posts or pillars and then extending the line of uprights and horizontals. This is known as the post-and-lintel method. It places heavy stresses on the lintel, which has to be strong enough not to bend or break under the weight of the building above it. The lintels have to be relatively short, which means that the interior space of the building is restricted by rows of closely placed pillars. Roman architects overcame the limitations of the post-and-lintel system by developing the arch (see pages 82–83).

Concrete: A technical breakthrough
In addition to the arch, the Romans made another important architectural innovation: the use of concrete. In some structures of the Hellenistic period builders used mortar or

The Romans mastered the arch, which made it possible to construct long aqueduct bridges such as this one, the Pont du Gard, in France. Built during the reign of Augustus, the aqueduct carried water across the Gard River to Nemausus (Nîmes).

cement (lime mixed with sand and water) to hold small stones together, but this was unusual in the ancient world. The Romans, however, made a startling discovery. They found that by mixing a particular kind of volcanic sand or ash, known as *pozzuolana*, with water, lime, and a hard aggregate (they often used broken tiles), they produced a very tough but adaptable building material—concrete.

At first Roman builders used concrete, mixed with rubble, as the interior filling of stone-faced walls. But later they used it on its own. It was cheaper and much stronger than stone, especially when large spaces had to be bridged. For example, it would have been impossible to build the Pantheon (see page 82) without concrete. For the lower walls, the Pantheon's builders used a mixture of concrete and travertine, a tough building stone quarried near Rome. The temple's dome was made up of concrete mixed with lighter volcanic rocks—tufa and pumice—to lessen the weight bearing down on the walls. The Romans also found that their *pozzuolana* concrete hardened under water, and they used it to construct baths and *naumachiae* (the artificial lakes used to stage mock naval battles).

Aqueducts
Roman engineers excelled in planning and constructing complex systems of aqueducts (water channels) to supply cities with drinking water. Rome had 19 aqueducts, from 10 to 60 miles (16 to 96 km) in length. The first was built in 312 BCE and the last in 226 CE, five centuries later. Eight of these aqueducts delivered about 220 million gallons (830 million liters) a day to the city, which amounts to 110–20 gallons (410–50 liters) per day per person. The New York City system today, by comparison, provides about 130 gallons (490 liters) per person daily.

One Roman soldier and engineer, Frontinus (c. 40–103 CE), was very proud of the aqueducts he engineered. He proclaimed, "Will anybody compare the idle Pyramids, or those other useless though renowned works of the Greeks with these aqueducts, with these many

Continues on page 84

THE ROMAN ARCH

The arch was the distinguishing feature of Roman architecture. An arch can carry a much greater load than other supporting structures because the weight of the building it supports pushes the arch's stones together instead of apart. The arch gave Roman architects freedom to build in a greater variety of ways. Arches could be strung together end-to-end to create a bridge across a valley. They could be placed side-by-side to create a curved roof or vault. Finally, the form of an arch could be turned through 360 degrees about its vertical axis so that it spanned a complete circle to create a dome.

Most Roman buildings are made up of a combination of arches, vaults, and domes—the Colosseum in Rome is an excellent example. In some buildings, a single form of the arch dominates. The great dome of the Pantheon in Rome, built between 120 and 124 CE, spans nearly 164 feet (50 m). It is wider than the dome of St. Peter's Basilica in Rome, which was built in the 16th century.

To make an arch, builders first constructed a curved wooden scaffolding between two pillars. They then built up the arch by placing carefully shaped stones along the curve of the scaffold. In the center and at the top, they positioned a heavier block, known as the keystone. The downward thrust (weight) of the keystone, and of the building above it, was transferred through the arch to the supporting pillars on either side, compressing and locking the other stones into place. Once the scaffolding was removed, the arch would stay in place for years or even centuries.

Expertise in constructing arches helped Roman architects to build the Pantheon, with its enormous dome. Erected by the emperor Hadrian in 120–24 CE to honor all the Roman gods, the Pantheon can still be seen in Rome today.

The arch gave rise to more complex forms, such as the cross vault and barrel vault, opening up new possibilities for the Roman architect.

Barrel vault

Cross vault

Arch

One of the finest achievements of Roman architecture was Rome's Colosseum (80 CE), which balances rows of arches one above the other. The building was 165 feet (50 m) high to the top of its fourth story, and took 20 years to complete.

82

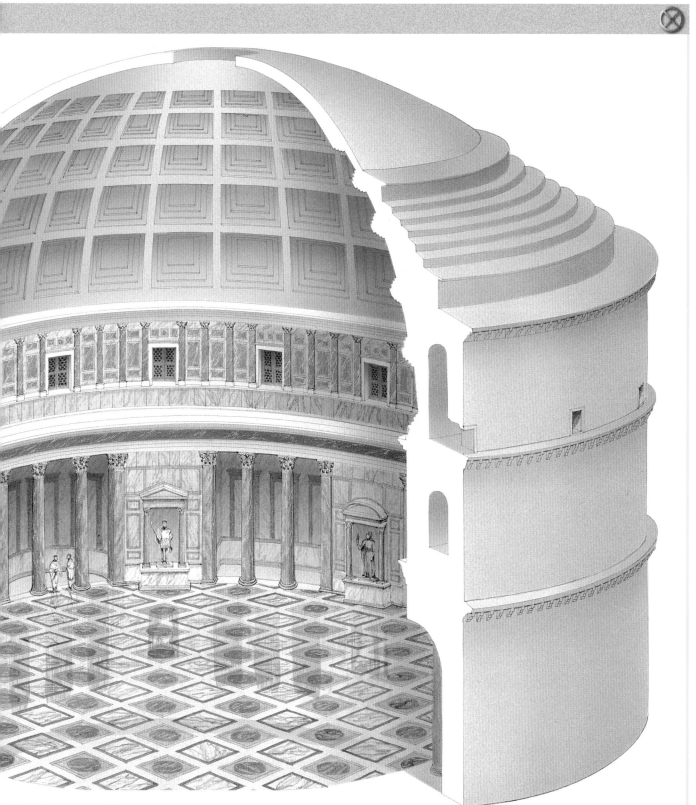

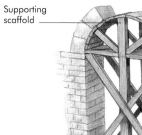

Supporting
scaffold

Keystone

*An arch can support
itself only when complete, so
builders used a scaffold to support
the weight of the arch until the
keystone—which locks together the
other stones—could be put in place.*

indispensable structures?" He had reason to boast, for elements of Roman aqueduct design are very impressive.

Water flowed through an aqueduct by gravity, so engineers ensured that an aqueduct followed a downhill gradient from water source to city. For most of an aqueduct's length, water flowed through a rectangular channel of stone or brick lined with a watertight cement. This channel was cut into the ground and covered with stone slabs to keep out dirt. Tunnels carried the channel through hills, and multi-arched bridges carried it across steep valleys.

If engineers wanted to avoid the expense of building long bridges across valleys, they created an inverted siphon to carry the water in lead pipes down one side of the valley, across a much shorter bridge and up the other side of the valley. As long as the water leaving the valley was at a lower level than the water coming into the valley, water pressure would push the water along the pipes and out of the valley. The only challenge was the strain placed on the pipes. The inverted siphon at Alatri, 50 miles (80 km) east of Rome, built around 134 BCE, had a vertical drop of 340 feet (116 m) and used a pipe 3.9 inches (10 cm) in diameter. This meant that the pressure was about 150 pounds per square inch

Their numerous *insulae* (apartment blocks) gave Roman cities a jumbled, cramped appearance, as shown in this 1st-century BCE relief. Some of these rickety structures were six stories tall and housed as many as 400 people.

(9 kg per sq. cm). Although the Romans routinely made lead pipes to carry water under city streets, it is not understood how Roman engineers made pipes that could handle the high pressures created in the siphon.

THE WORLD OF THE CITY

The wealthy Roman citizen lived in a luxurious *domus* (townhouse). Much of what we know about this type of building comes from studies of Pompeii, the Roman town buried and preserved beneath lava and ash when the volcano Mount Vesuvius erupted in 79 CE.

⊗ TOWN PLANNING

The Romans built dozens of new cities throughout their expanding empire from north Africa to Britain. These cities often began as military encampments or garrisons, or as colonies for former soldiers, but imperial administrators and merchants soon joined the soldiers. The trappings of Roman civilization also attracted local peoples. Native leaders were often granted Roman citizenship and public office, which gave them a stake in the affairs of the empire. Urbanization thus helped to absorb conquered peoples into the Roman empire.

These new settlements all followed the same regular pattern (although the planners made some concessions to local climate and geography). Planners laid out each settlement in a rectangle enclosed by strong walls with only four gates. Two main avenues

connected gates on either side of the city, a custom that the Romans adopted from the Etruscans, while secondary streets were laid out at right angles to each other, forming square blocks. In the city's center, the Romans created an open plaza, or forum for civic and religious events.

The main building in the forum was the temple. Temples were imposing buildings, raised on a high platform to dominate the area around them and approached up a flight of steps. They were used by priests and officials for the set rituals of the official Roman religion. Most Roman cities boasted an amphitheater (for public entertainments), and public baths. There might also be a theater—such as the one still standing at Orange, in southern France, today—as well as a triumphal arch.

1. Ornamental pool
2. *Atrium*
3. Living room
4. Dining room
5. Kitchen
6. Bedrooms
7. Main staircase
8. Servants' quarters
9. Upper dining room
10. *Peristylium,* colonnaded garden
11. Household shrine
12. Shop

This cutaway view of a Roman *domus* (townhouse) shows the luxurious home life enjoyed by the upper classes. The *peristylium,* or colonnaded garden, gave the house an air of spaciousness—in contrast to the cramped conditions of the *insulae,* apartment blocks where the poor lived.

Roman townhouses faced inward and were built around a central courtyard, or *atrium*. To ensure privacy none of the windows looked onto the street; light and air came through an opening in the roof above the *atrium*, and rainwater was collected in an ornamental pool in the center. Several rooms surrounded the *atrium*: *cubicula* (bedrooms), the *tablinum* where the master of the house could receive guests, the *triclinium*, or family dining room, and the kitchen. The front rooms of houses were often rented out as shops. The upstairs rooms might include a library as well as servants' quarters. At the rear was the *peristylium*, a garden with covered walkways and sometimes a fountain.

Romans generally had few pieces of furniture. Household goods were stored in niches or wooden cupboards. Diners reclined on couches to eat and took food from low tables; the best dishes would be displayed on the sideboard. Well-off Romans had carpets, paintings, curtains, and lamp stands, while the homes of the truly wealthy were embellished with statues and elaborate floor mosaics. In less-wealthy homes, there might be only a few chairs and a table. Cutlery and plates in these homes were made of bronze and pottery instead of silver, which was used by the wealthy.

Apartment blocks

Most people in the cities, however, could not afford to own a *domus*, and instead rented an apartment in a large building known as an *insula* (plural *insulae*), which usually had shops and other businesses at ground level. Many *insulae* stood five or six stories tall. Each room on the upper floors was entered by its own exterior wooden staircase. The larger and more expensive rooms were on the lower floors.

The *insulae* of Rome were scandalously overcrowded. Many had been poorly built and they frequently caught fire or collapsed under the weight of their numerous inhabitants. In addition, the rents charged in Rome were often 10 times higher than those in other cities, and conditions for the poorest people were appalling. In 64 CE, after a terrible fire destroyed much of Rome, the emperor Nero (reigned 54–68) took action to limit some of the worst problems of the *insulae*. Regulations prohibited shoddy construction, put a limit on the maximum height of *insulae*, and required buildings to be separated from one another by a large enough space to prevent fires from spreading.

After Rome was rebuilt, *insulae* continued to provide most of the housing. By the 4th century CE the city contained 44,000 *insulae* and only 1,800 *domus*.

Fountains and baths

While a few wealthy people had water supplied directly to their homes, the vast majority of Romans got their water from fountains located throughout the city. At its height, Rome had 1,352 fountains and basins, 15 *nymphaea* (monumental fountains), two *naumachiae* (artificial lakes), 11 *thermae* (hot baths), and 856 public baths.

A visit to the public baths was a central feature of everyday life for all Roman citizens. Roman baths were not just places for getting clean or for exercising–people also came there to relax, talk, do business, and make social contacts, and the complex of buildings included gymnasiums, lounges, and snack bars.

The baths themselves were constructed following a similar pattern. At the entrance were changing rooms, followed by a *caldarium* (hot room), a *tepidarium* (moderately heated room), a *frigidarium* (cold room), and finally a *natatio* (swimming pool). Much like present-day spas, the baths also had rooms for saunas and massages. In the *unctuaria*, slaves oiled and scraped the bathers' bodies with polished iron implements called *strigils*, and removed their body hair.

At the Forum baths of Pompeii, hot air circulating through vents kept the *caldarium* hot. Bathers would splash themselves with cold water from the basin at the rear.

Underfloor heating

The Romans used an underfloor system called a hypocaust to heat rooms in the baths. The floor of the room was built over a cavity and supported on piles of terracotta bricks or tiles. Flues, built into the walls of the cavity, created a draft that drew hot air, heated by a fire in an adjoining room, under the floor, where it circulated around the piles. The floor of the heated room was laid with terracotta tiles, which are excellent conductors of heat; sometimes the heated floor was so hot that bathers had to wear wooden clogs to protect their feet.

The fire for the hypocaust also heated the bath in the *caldarium*. A small section of the bath floor was made particularly thin so that it could be heated by the hot air circulating beneath it. This part of the floor was divided off from the main pool to prevent bathers from burning their

Outer wall

Box-flue tiles

Foundations

HOUSEHOLD ARTICLES

The Romans were ingenious in designing tools and implements for all kinds of domestic purposes. Often the basic idea came from outside but the Romans improved and refined it. Crude scissors were first used in ancient Egypt, for example, but Roman scissors were more sophisticated and could be used for a variety of tasks, including cutting out garments. The Romans were the first to use a brace-and-bit for drilling. They designed locks that used keys to secure doors, cupboards, and trunks. They had the first candles made from rendered animal fat (tallow) molded around a wick of vegetable fiber.

Romans were quick to see new uses for things in daily life. For instance, they used a mixture of animal tallow, ashes, and red herbs as a hair dye and healing ointment, but later in the 4th

This bronze lock and key date from the late 1st or early 2nd century CE.

century discovered that it could be used as a soap to clean skin and clothes. Glass bottles and jars were widely used for oils, cosmetics, and perfumes in Roman homes.

Glassblowing, invented in Syria in the 1st century BCE, became a major industry in the Roman empire. Glassmakers attached a mass of molten glass to a blowpipe and then inflated and shaped it. They were particularly skilled at cutting glass to form cameo reliefs. Vessels were often made from two layers of glass, usually dark blue and white. Skilled craftsmen then carved the white layer into elaborate designs and patterns, cutting right through it in places to reveal the blue glass underneath.

feet. The water heated by convection—as water warms, it becomes less dense and rises, and cold water sinks to take its place.

Hypocausts were expensive, requiring elaborate construction and frequent repairs, and so were used only in the public baths or the homes of the wealthy. At some point during the 4th century CE, Romans began heating their homes using a fireplace and chimney similar to those found in modern buildings.

Street life

Because of their often limited living accommodations, urban Romans spent much of the day away from home, going to the baths or sporting events at the amphitheaters, or visiting the forum to do business, sacrifice at the temple, or catch up on the latest political gossip. Shops, or *tabernae*, lined the streets of a Roman city, offering a wide range of goods and services. There were pharmacies, cabinetmakers, jewelers, bakeries, shoemakers, barbers, laundries, and banks, to name a few. Peddlers hawked goods and food on the street, and there were taverns for drinking and gambling.

Lively by day, Roman streets were dark and dangerous at night, and people generally avoided going out after sunset. If they had to

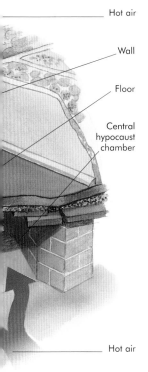

The hypocaust was an early form of central heating. Hot air from a furnace flowed under the floor and escaped through flues in the walls.

— Hot air

— Wall

— Floor

Central hypocaust chamber

— Hot air

A layer of volcanic ash preserved much of Pompeii after Mount Vesuvius erupted in 79 CE. This street in Pompeii—lined with workshops, taverns, food outlets, and homes, all in close proximity to one another—was typical of Roman towns.

venture out at night, Romans traveled in groups for safety, often with a slave going ahead and carrying a lantern.

To try to lessen Rome's heavy traffic, the authorities banned private carts from entering the city by day unless they were carrying garbage or building materials for public projects. People left their horses and vehicles at parking lots just outside the city.

A corps of watchmen, known as *vigiles,* served as firefighters. In addition to ladders and buckets, the *vigile*s had pumps that drew water from the public fountains. These pumps used a piston to suck water into a chamber and then into a nozzle, a principle that is used in many modern pumps.

CLOTHING

The Romans principally used woolen cloth and linen for clothing and other household purposes. They also used felt and leather. They made few improvements to spinning and weaving technologies, though in the late empire they began to use a comb to separate the fibers before spinning them.

For much of the Roman period, the basic garment for both men and women was the sleeveless and tight-waisted *tunica*. It was knee- or calf-length and for important individuals was decorated with a strip of purple along its bottom edge. For men, the *tunica* was completed by the addition of a toga, a large white woolen cloak that wrapped in folds around the body, leaving the right arm free. For women, the *tunica* was completed by adding the *stola*, a short-sleeved dress—often dyed red, yellow, green, or blue—that was fastened at the waist by a belt and draped to form pleats.

As the empire grew wealthier, women wore gold jewelry, cosmetics, and elaborate hairstyles. As Pliny the Elder observed in the 1st century CE, "People nowadays go to buy clothes in China, look for pearls in the depths of the Red Sea, and emeralds in the bowels of the earth. Moreover, the practice of piercing has been invented: it evidently did not suffice to wear jewels round the neck, in the hair or on the hands; they also have to be stuck in the body."

North of the Alps, Romans wore clothing better suited to the cold climate, adopted from the Gauls and Germans—trousers, tunics, hooded

mantles, socks, and laced boots, with outer garments made of furs. To fasten this type of clothing, people used *fibulae*, hinged or spring-loaded pins (buttons were used for decoration only). In the last centuries of the empire, Romans throughout the Western provinces wore this European style of dress.

CRISIS AND DECLINE

In the 2nd century plagues swept the Roman empire, killing a large part of the population and seriously disrupting economic life. With fewer people available to farm the land, there were food shortages in the cities and reduced tax revenues. The drop in manpower also caused a

Fine clothes and elaborate hairstyles are evident in this wall painting from Herculaneum, one of the cities buried in ash when the volcano Mount Vesuvius erupted in 79 CE. A slave combs a girl's hair (right) while the lady of the house and her other daughter look on (left).

centuries were nearly always military commanders from one of the provinces.

As the economic situation worsened in the 3rd century, the problem of succession became more violent and divisive. The result was a series of weak emperors who were not up to the task of reviving Roman society. Few ever visited the capital for long. Removed from the center of power, the aristocratic families of Rome were no longer interested in political or military service for the common good, but looked to their own concerns. To the Roman populace, despondent over the downward spiral of their culture, life seemed difficult and ultimately futile. Many Roman tombstones of the time ended with the epitaph, "I was, I was not, I am not, I don't care."

Using technology to slow the decline
In these difficult times, the Romans turned one last time to technology. The idea of using the water of a fast-moving stream to turn the paddles of a wheel was known to the Greeks, but the Romans had made little use of water power until the 4th century CE. In an attempt to provide sufficient flour for the urban masses, the Romans began using waterwheels to power grain mills. One example was the enormous water-powered

Roman engineers harnessed water power in spectacular fashion at Barbegal, France, where 16 waterwheels turned millstones to grind flour.

shortfall of army recruits and, as the cash crisis mounted, the army often went unpaid for long periods. It became ever more difficult to maintain troops on the frontier to meet the constant threat of invasion from the Germanic tribes living on the empire's northern fringes.

Compounding these problems was a decline in leadership and civic virtue. The Romans had never established a reliable pattern of imperial succession. Although most emperors tried to designate their successor, their choice was by no means assured. A powerful rival frequently upset the succession process by gaining the loyalty of the army, who would force the senate to name their choice as emperor. Consequently, emperors in the later mill at Barbegal near Arles, France. This mill employed 16 wheels fed by water from the local aqueduct, and its millstones could grind about 28 tons of grain a day. The total energy generated by the wheels has been estimated at between 32 and 64 horsepower, making Barbegal the largest power installation in the ancient world.

Dividing the empire

One emperor did attempt to halt the empire's decline–Diocletian (reigned 284–305). He divided the empire into four areas of military responsibility, and shared the administration with three co-rulers. He improved the tax system, refortified the frontiers, and increased the size of the army.

Some 20 years after Diocletian's death, Constantine the Great (reigned 324–337) made himself emperor of the Roman world after defeating a rival, Licinius. Constantine founded a new eastern capital at Byzantium on the Bosporus, the strait that divides Europe from Asia, and named it Constantinople (modern-day Istanbul). From then on, the empire increasingly functioned as two parts. In 395 this division was made permanent, with a Western empire ruled from Rome and an Eastern empire ruled from Constantinople.

Barbarian success

The Roman empire was not the only apparently secure and prosperous empire to face external pressure in the early 1st millennium CE. Repeated nomadic raids from central Asia contributed to the break-up of the 400-year-old Han dynasty of China in the 2nd century CE (see this volume: Early China). Historians believe that a series of famines in the late 4th century caused a major wave of migration among the nomadic peoples of the steppes of central Asia, creating widening ripples of disturbance and threatening the stability of the settled regions at the periphery. In the 5th and 6th centuries the Roman empire, the Gupta empire of northern India, and the Sassanian empire of Persia were all attacked by Turkic invaders, variously known as Huns, Ephthalite (White) Huns, and Avars.

As the Huns pushed west into the Balkans and eastern Europe, they displaced Germanic tribes (called Barbarians by the Romans) that had long been living on the frontiers of the empire. Some of the Germanic tribes turned to

Successive invasions of the Western empire by Germanic tribes reached a climax in 476, when the Barbarian general Odoacer deposed the last Western emperor. The empire in the West ceased to exist, apart from a short-lived state in Dalmatia, and its former provinces were divided into a number of Barbarian kingdoms. The Eastern empire developed into the Byzantine empire, which lasted until 1493.

Invaders of the empire

invasion routes of barbarians
- → Angles, Saxons and Jutes
- → Britons
- → Franks

territories at 476 CE
- kingdom of Soissons
- Burgundian kingdom
- Visigothic kingdom
- Vandal kingdom
- kingdom of Odoacer
- Western Roman empire
- Eastern Roman empire

Rome for protection and were given land on which to settle within the empire, in return for military service. Under a succession of weak emperors, the Barbarians began carving up kingdoms for themselves in Gaul, Spain, and north Africa. In 476 CE Odoacer, a Barbarian general, deposed Romulus Augustulus, the last Roman emperor in the West, and was crowned king of Italy by his soldiers.

The Eastern empire–wealthier and more populous than the Western empire–was better able to withstand the Germanic impact. As the Byzantine empire it lasted for another 1,000 years before falling to the Ottoman Turks in 1453.

THE LEGACY OF THE ROMANS

As the Germanic kings took control of territory once ruled by Rome, they adopted the ideas and practices of their predecessors, including Latin and Christianity. As a result, Latin came to shape the new languages of western Europe–Italian, French, Spanish, and Portuguese–and influenced others (many English words have Latin roots). The Christian Church had already adopted elements of Roman administration such as the dioceses (administrative districts) introduced by Diocletian. Bishops were often headquartered in Roman provincial cities and towns, giving continuity to urban life in many parts of the empire. Roman law continued to serve as the basis for law throughout much of Europe.

In terms of technology, the Romans also left a legacy, both large and small. We continue to marvel at their cities, roads, and monuments. They anticipated many of the things we take for granted in daily life, pioneering their own versions of indoor plumbing and heating, pumps, candles, scissors, even soap. The Romans drew on a wide range of ideas and shaped them into technology that served their beliefs and values.

Many Barbarian groups quickly adopted Roman ways. The Vandals, for example, made their way through Gaul and Spain before crossing the sea to north Africa, where they settled on the grain-rich lands around Carthage. This early 6th-century mosaic from Carthage shows a Vandal nobleman setting out from his villa on a hunting expedition, just as the Roman landowner who lived there before him would have done.

91

Index

Page numbers in *italic* type refer to picture captions. **Bold** page numbers refer to the main discussion of the subject.

Liyi (China) 28–29
Sanxingdui (China) 12
terracotta army 12, **28–29**

F

farming
in China **12–16**
dry farming 74
dry-field farming 12
fertilization 14
husking 15
improvements in 14–15
ox-drawn harvesters *74, 75*
rotation of crops 14
row cultivation 14–15
seed-drills 15
winnowing fans 15
see also agriculture
feasts, ritual, in China 16
firefighting, in Rome 88
First Dark Age 47, 50
trade revival after 51
flood prevention in mining 76
flour mills, water-powered, in China 16
food, in China **12–16**
forging (of metals) 23, 45, 48
Forum (Rome) *71, 72*
fountains, Roman 86
Frontinus 81–84
furnaces, blast 23, *48*

G

galleys (ships) 78
Gaugamela, Battle of *61*
gladius (sword) 67
glassblowing, Roman 87
glass
Phoenician *51, 53*
trade 39
gold
Scythian nomads *47*
trade 38
Grand Canal (China) 34–35
Great Wall of China 30–31
Greece
alphabet, early 55
architecture 59
art 58

city-states 53, 57–58, 60–61
classical 53–60
medicine 59–60
philosophy 58–59
pottery *57*
science 58
technological adaptation 53
theater 58
trade 53
warfare 53–57
writing 47, 58

H

Hadrian's Wall 68
hammers, water–driven 15
handmills 16
Han dynasty (China) 11, 22
iron and steel working 24
overthrow of 34
harbors, Roman 78
harness *see under* horses
harvester, ox-drawn *74, 75*
Hattusas 44
heating, underfloor, Roman 86–87
Hebrews 50
Hellenistic world 61–63
Hero of Alexandria 63
Hippocrates 60
Hittites 36, **44–47**
collapse of empire 47
trade 45
Homer 50, 58
honey 38
hoplites 53
horizontal draw looms 26
horses
breaststrap harness 32
domestication of 12, 46
introduction into China 12
riding 46
on Roman roads 78
Houma (China), bronze foundry 20
houses, Roman 85–86
Huns 12, 47, 90
hypocausts 86–87

I

Iliad 50
Ionian Greeks 50
Iron Age *see* Early Iron Age
iron production
in China 12, **23–24**
in Mediterranean lands 51
iron, white 23
ironworking
Hittite 45–47
Mediterranean **48–49**
irrigation
in China 32–34
paddy fields 12–13
Israelites 50
ivory 38, 52

J

jade *26, 27*
javelin (Roman) 69
jia *15*
Jiaohe *33*
Julius Caesar 70

K

Khania 42
Knossos **42–43**

L

lacquerware, in China 25
Lake Fucino tunnel (Italy) 72
lakes, artificial 72, 81, 86
land ownership, in China 13–14
lapis lazuli 38, 45
Latin (language) 91
alphabet, early *55*
Latins (people) 64
legions 67
Linear A script 41
Linear B script 44, 47, 54
Livy 64
Liyi (China) 28–29
looms, horizontal draw 26
lost-wax casting method *18*
lumber trade 45, 52
luxury goods, in China 24–26

M

Macedonians 60–61
"Magic Canal" (China) 33
malleable cast iron 24
Mallia 42
manuballista 68
mass production
bronze 19, 20
in early China 12, 15, 19
lacquerware 25
pottery 19, 28
mathematics 58, 59
medicine, in Greece 59–60
Mediterranean regions
ancient **36–63**
timeline **36–37**
trade in 38–39
Meng Tian 30
merchant ships, Roman 78
metallurgy, Roman 76
metals, trade and transportation in the Mediterranean 39
millet, in China 11, 12, 15
mining
flood prevention 76
in Roman empire 76
Minoans 38, **39–41**
earthquakes/volcano destruction 41
legends about 44
pottery 42
technology **42–43**
trade 39, 41, **42–43**
writing 41
Minos 44
mirrors, war *62*
modular production
in early China 19, 25, 28
lacquerware 25
pottery 19, 28
music
in China 16–19
mechanical, in Rome 72
Mycenaeans 38, **41–44**
conquest of Crete 41
legends about 44
trade 38–39
writing 44

Picture credits